CONFLICT TO CONNECTION

A Blueprint to Find Peace Amidst Chaos

Sunita Khadanga

INDIA • SINGAPORE • MALAYSIA

ISBN 979-8-89067-928-4

Contents

Acknowledgements

I extend my heartfelt gratitude to my parents, Geeta Khadanga and Durga Prasad Khadanga, who have been the pillars of strength in my life's journey. My sisters, Sandhya and Sagarika, have been my unwavering support system, inspiring and encouraging me at every step. I owe a special thanks to Mr. Rakesh Shukla (ISRO), whose continuous support, guidance, and encouragement have been instrumental in my pursuits. Lastly, I want to thank my friends, who have always believed in me and stood by my side. This journey would not have been possible without each one of you. Thank you.

"As wind chimes to a breeze, love sways to the heart's gentle touch"

– Sunita Khadanga

CHAPTER 1

Unraveling the Threads of Relationships

"The quality of your life is the quality of your relationships."

– Tony Robbins

Life, with its myriad hues and textures, is akin to a vast tapestry, a grand theatre of human emotions. At its core, it's not about the great monoliths of events that tower over the landscape of our days, but about the intimate interweavings of individual threads that give it its vibrancy and life. These threads, many-hued and vibrant, are the intricate relationships we build, nurture, and sometimes let go of, in the vast panorama of our existence.

This is the real narrative of life in the Indian subcontinent, a place where relationships are not just an important part of life, but are life itself. In this part of the world, the self is not isolated. Rather, it is deeply rooted in an intricate meshwork of relationships, each thread carrying its own story of love, sacrifice, joy, pain, and growth.

The culture, with its rich and colourful tapestry, forms a striking backdrop to these stories. It is a vibrant palette of customs, traditions, languages, and values that have been passed down through generations. The collective wisdom of a civilization that has been writing its story for thousands of years whispers through every interaction, every ritual, every smile, and every tear.

A stroll through the streets of any Indian city is a study in contrast and harmony, a silent play that brings this grand theatre of relationships to life. The old and the new coexist, stories of the past intertwining with dreams of the future, with relationships forming the firmament that holds it all together.

A grandmother, sitting on a traditional wooden swing, her wrinkled hands weaving stories of the past as her young granddaughter listens, rapt. The local chai-wallah, with his mobile tea stall, serves more than just steaming cups of tea. He serves familiarity, a constant in the ever-changing urban landscape, as regular patrons, from auto-rickshaw drivers to software engineers, exchange tales of their lives over their daily cuppa. A young woman, balancing the weight of tradition and modernity, navigates the nuances of a new professional relationship in a globally-connected Indian firm. A couple shares a lingering look, love blossoming amidst the chaos of a city that is always on the move.

Here, relationships are not just interactions, but a mirror of the culture itself, a reflection of its past, its present, and its hopes for the future. They embody the richness of Indian ethos, the soul of its people, the rhythms of its heart. And it is in the heart of this theatre, on this stage of relationships, that the human emotions dance to the tunes of joy and sorrow, love and heartbreak, growth and loss.

Take, for example, the dynamics within the Indian family structure. These are not just households, they are mini-universities of human emotions, nurseries of the self, where one learns the first steps of the dance of life. Each family, a little cosmos of its own, is a world filled with myriad relationships – between parents and children, between siblings, between the old and the young, and between the human and the divine.

In these households, traditions are not relics of the past, they are living, breathing entities that make their presence felt in everyday life. Morning prayers, the lighting of the oil lamp, the intricate art of Rangoli, the aroma of the freshly-ground spices wafting from the kitchen – each is a silent nod to the continuity of traditions that weave together the story of the family.

However, tradition here is not a monolith. It is an ever-evolving entity, constantly in dialogue with the winds of change. The modern Indian household is not just a keeper of traditions but is also a cauldron of transformation, where the old and new blend seamlessly.

Witness a mother, who tells tales from the ancient epics to her children at night, but also encourages them to question, to seek, and to learn from the world. A father, who wants his children to respect their roots, but also to spread their wings and embrace the sky. A teenager, balancing the scales of identity – cherishing her traditional Indian wear but also taking delight in the latest global fashion trends. The story of the Indian family is a testament to the harmony that can exist between tradition and modernity if we dare to explore and engage.

From the household, let us step into the urban jungle of the modern Indian professional world. Here, relationships take on a different hue, reflecting the aspirations, competitiveness, and resilience of a new India. As the country continues to be a global player, the Indian professional navigate relationships that are not just local but also global, a dance that requires grace, understanding, and adaptability.

From personal relationships woven within the cosy corners of our homes to professional interactions that straddle across skyscrapers touching the Indian sky, to romantic exchanges that breathe life into poetry, songs, and a billion beating hearts – the dance of relationships in India is a spectacle to behold, an experience to be lived, a story to be told. And so, we embark on this journey, to delve into the depths of these relationships, to understand the conflicts that arise, to appreciate their value, and to learn from their resilience. For it is in understanding these relationships that we understand India, and in the process, we understand a little more about the vastness and beauty of the human experience itself.

This book, much like a deftly woven pashmina, attempts to unravel these intricacies. Each thread, a story of a relationship, will lead us on a journey through the three important arenas of human relationships – the personal, the professional, and the romantic. It is a voyage that will take us to the intimate corners of Indian homes, into the bustling corporate offices, and through the winding lanes of romance.

The personal sphere is where our journey begins, navigating the serpentine path of familial relationships and friendships. We step into the close-knit Indian families, where the elderly and the young coexist, traditions and modernity intertwine, and love and conflict often dance hand in hand. We delve into the sacred bond of friendship that sees no barriers of age, gender, or class, and often transcends the limitations of family.

From the personal, we move into the professional arena. The Indian work milieu, a rich potpourri of diverse cultures, languages, and ideologies, forms a fascinating backdrop to this narrative. Here, relationships are born out of necessity, moulded by ambition, and often tested by conflict. Amidst the maze of corporate politics, we learn to negotiate, collaborate, compete, and often, to survive.

Our voyage then sails into the tumultuous sea of romantic relationships. In a land where love is celebrated with a fervour unmatched – from the immortal love stories etched in its ancient scriptures to the vibrant depiction of romance in Bollywood cinema, love and relationships occupy a significant space in the Indian psyche. Yet, the path of love, as it unfolds in the real lives of people, is not always as rosy. Through the triumphs and trials of romantic relationships, we witness the poignant dance of love, heartbreak, reconciliation, and growth.

As we embark on this exploratory journey, we shall witness the intricate interplay of emotions, expectations, and identities in these relationships. We shall encounter conflicts, those uninvited guests, that bring unrest, but often leave behind a deeper understanding and a stronger bond. We shall learn to see these conflicts not as disruptors, but as catalysts that foster growth and resilience.

This journey is not just an exploration of relationships and conflicts within them; it is also a celebration of these relationships. A celebration of their complexity, their dynamism, and their capacity to shape and transform us. For, as we journey through these relationships, we realize that they are not just part of our lives, they are the tapestry that makes up our life. As we delve deeper, we begin to see the beauty and strength of the threads that hold this tapestry together, and how they colour our existence with their unique hues. And in doing so, we come to appreciate the real grandeur of the Indian theatre of relationships, a theatre that is as enchanting, as diverse, and as resilient as India itself.

CHAPTER 2

The Inevitable Dance of Conflict

"Peace is not the absence of conflict, it is the ability to handle conflict by peaceful means."

– Ronald Reagan

In the ballad of relationships, there is a character that often goes unacknowledged. Like an enigmatic dancer veiled behind layers of silken fabric, it sways and weaves its way through the intricate steps of our bonds. This mysterious figure, this uninvited guest, is Conflict.

Ah, conflict – the very word has an unsettling resonance to it, a murmur that ruffles the still waters of our hearts. It's as if a shadow crosses the room every time the word is spoken, and the air turns heavy with an unsaid tension. In the Indian society, where relationships are often perceived as sacrosanct, the admission of conflict is akin to a blight upon the fabric of our bonds.

But what if we were to stop for a moment and gently lift the veil? What if we were to unmask conflict, to look into its eyes without prejudice or fear? We would find, dear reader, that conflict is not just an intruder; it is a companion, a fellow traveller in our relational journeys.

Like the spice in our curries, conflict lends our relationships flavours – sometimes too strong, sometimes subtle, but always undeniable. It is not to be shunned but embraced and understood.

Conflict's dance is ancient and universal, but within the vivid tableau of Indian culture, its steps take on a myriad of hues. Here, conflict does not just arise from opposing desires or clashing egos; it is often a ripple in the deep ocean of traditions, roles, and expectations that surround Indian relationships.

Imagine a kitchen in an old Indian home. The scent of turmeric and coriander wafts through the air as two women – a mother-in-law and a daughter-in-law – move around each other like seasoned dancers. But, in this dance, there is tension. An heirloom recipe, handed down through generations, becomes a silent battleground. A missing pinch of salt, a variation in method – it's not just about taste; it is about tradition, about legacies. This is a subtle conflict, one that does not speak loudly but sings in undertones.

Take another stage – an Indian office. A young, ambitious woman's drive for innovation collides with her senior colleague's firm hold on convention. Theirs is a conflict wrapped in the pages of reports and proposals, but it is, in essence, a tussle between change and tradition, between the old guard and the new.

Conflict is not always the roiling storm; sometimes it is the gentle breeze that nudges us toward reflection and growth. It challenges the status quo, provokes introspection, and sometimes, yes, it leads to heartache. But, would the pages of our lives be as rich, as resonant, without the brushstrokes of conflict to give them depth?

Let us not be deceived, however, into thinking that the dance of conflict is always graceful or benign. There are times when conflict storms into the ballroom of our lives like a tempest, leaving havoc in its wake. But here too, even in the eye of the storm, there is something to be learned, something to be salvaged.

Imagine a young couple in love, from different castes or religious backgrounds. Their love is tender, their dreams interwoven like fingers clasped in the moonlight.

But the world around them swirls with voices – voices of tradition, of prejudice, of societal norms. Their conflict with their families and society becomes a defining crucible, one that will either shatter them or forge them into something stronger. This is a conflict that raises questions beyond the personal, beckoning the collective conscience of a culture. It asks – what is the worth of love? How much can it bear? And when is it time to break the chains that bind?

In a small village, a father's dreams for his daughter clash against the glass ceiling of patriarchal norms. She is bright, her eyes fixed on horizons yet unseen. But the path is littered with thorns of resistance. This is not just her conflict; it is the echo of countless dreams caged behind closed doors. Here, conflict has the power to become a catalyst for change, a bridge that connects yesterday's sacrifices to tomorrow's revolutions.

As we unveil the complexities of interpersonal dynamics, we come to understand that conflicts are as intricate as the varied landscapes they unfold in. India, with its diverse tapestry of cultures, languages, and belief systems, provides a fertile ground for conflicts to simmer and flourish.

But conflict is not an end; it is often a beginning – of conversations, of realizations, of revolutions. It is not just a guest, but a traveller who takes us on paths unknown. In its wake, we find broken chains, but also new bonds. Through its lens, we see not just the cracks, but also the mosaic that is our lives.

In this journey, dear reader, we must learn to dance with conflict. To understand its steps, to move with grace through its twirls, and to sometimes let it lead. For, in this dance, we are not just participants; we are also choreographers. We have the power to shape the dance, to turn it from a storm into a symphony.

So let us not shun conflict, but invite it in. Let us talk with it, engage with it, and let us listen to the tales it has to tell. Here are two tales

Tales of heartache, yes, but also of hope; of shattered dreams, but also of new beginnings; of the yesteryears, but also of the possibilities that await.

For it is through these tales that we will traverse the landscape of relationships in all their complexity and beauty.

Whispering Corridors: Reflections on a Silent Turmoil

In the heart of Bangalore, where the skies are often a muted grey and the streets are woven with an energy that never slumbers, there stands a sleek building of glass and chrome. Its windows capture the city's reflections – a thousand dreams, a million heartbeats. Within these walls is an office, a microcosm of modern India, where technology and humanity entwine in a ceaseless dance.

Enter Rajeev – a man in his forties, clad in a crisp white shirt, the creases sharp enough to slice through the day. His spectacles perch on the bridge of his nose, a vantage point

from which he surveys his kingdom. His kingdom, though, is an open-plan office space. As a manager, he has been steering the ship for well over a decade, and he prides himself on being the compass that navigates through the corporate storm.

One fine morning, as the aroma of filter coffee wafts through the corridors, Rajeev's realm is graced by a new presence – Shreya. She is fresh out of college, with a smile that reaches her eyes and a walk that seems to compose melodies with the air. Her desk, a humble abode, is situated within eyeshot of Rajeev's cabin.

As the days pass, Shreya is like a breath of fresh air. She brings new ideas, unafraid of questioning the age-old ways. Her presentations are stories; her emails are akin to poetic conversations.

Rajeev, though appreciative of her talents, finds his feathers ruffled. Her unabashed approach uncovers the dormant layers of his insecurities. Her questions, though innocent, are like soft knocks on the doors he had closed long ago.

One mundane Tuesday, as the clock ticks its way through an afternoon that seems to stretch its limbs leisurely, a ripple moves through the office. A presentation Shreya has been working on is praised by the higher-ups, and her innovation is lauded.

The clattering keyboards suddenly sound like applause to Shreya but feel like rain on a tin roof to Rajeev.

The storm is subtle at first. Rajeev's words acquire an edge, his praise becomes scarce. The meetings become a battleground where passive-aggressive jabs are exchanged.

As weeks pass, the air between them thickens. The unspoken words, the unsaid apologies, and the unacknowledged fears hang heavily.

Rajeev, though initially appreciative of Shreya's zeal, soon finds himself in uncharted waters. Her fresh perspective, though innovative, often challenges the long-established practices he holds dear. Her questions, innocent yet pointed, prick at the bubble of his comfort zone, stirring up ripples of unease.

This undercurrent of tension begins to simmer, subtly altering the dynamics of their interactions. Meetings turn into a dance of diplomacy, while feedback sessions become a tightrope walk on the thin line between personal feelings and professional critique.

The air grows taut as the invisible strings of rivalry and insecurity are pulled tauter. Under the sterile glare of the fluorescent lights, the office becomes a stage for a subtle power play; a shadow theatre where the unsaid words cast longer shadows than what is spoken.

Let us peer a little closer into the brewing tempest in Rajeev's soul. Time, with its relentless tide, has etched lines onto his face and streaked his hair with silver. In Shreya's accolades, he hears the whispers of the aspirations he once cradled, the glimmers of a past where the future was a canvas yet to be painted. But the road has since been long, and the storms weathered have left him seeking refuge in the safety of the known. In the sanctuary of tried and tested waters, Rajeev had fortified himself against the winds of change.

But why does Shreya, this bright, unwavering flame, become the north wind that stirs the waves in Rajeev's tranquil harbour?

For Shreya, the world is still brimming with possibilities. Each morning she steps into the office with the zeal to carve her path. The gears of the corporate machinery, although new to her, represent challenges she is eager to embrace. However, as she stretches her wings, she finds the air thickening with restraint. The winds she wants to ride are laden with undercurrents she cannot fathom.

Shreya's exuberance, reflecting off the mirrors of the corporate tower, is unknowingly illuminating the alcoves of Rajeev's compromises and the silent resignation that had seeped into his bones. It is not mere envy that steers the ship of conflict, but a clashing of worlds – of what has been and what could be.

In the hallways, their footsteps sync to different rhythms, and their words, though seemingly harmonious, jostle like discordant notes.

The onlookers, the silent witnesses of this unfolding drama – the colleagues, the interns, the everyday faces that are the fabric of this corporate microcosm – begin to perceive the tension. They watch as the mentor who they respected, and the fledgling who brought hope, dance around each other in a waltz that neither understands.

A Wedding in Rajasthan

Amidst the golden dunes of Rajasthan, where the winds whisper ancient tales, the imposing silhouette of a majestic fort rises against the vermilion sky. Here, within walls that have seen countless suns rise and set, another story is being woven into the tapestry of time.

It is a celebration that makes the very air thrum with anticipation. The fort, clad in a myriad of lights, looks like a kingdom plucked from a storybook. The aroma of marigolds mingles with the scent of sumptuous delicacies that promise to satiate more than just the appetite.

In the embrace of this grandeur, we find Aarav – tall, with a smile that could tame the stars. His eyes carry the weight of generations; he is the scion of a family whose roots burrow deep into the land they call home.

Meera, a vision in red, walks with the grace of the moonlit night. Her laughter, as delicate as the tinkling of temple bells, masks a spirit both fierce and tender.

Aarav and Meera's wedding is the culmination of the dreams of two families, as old as the fort itself, seeking to forge a future together. The families had meticulously woven this alliance like artisans crafting a precious tapestry.

As the rituals commence, ancient customs cradle the couple. The sacred fire bears witness to promises made under a sky strewn with constellations.

But, as shadows and light play their eternal game within the fort, whispers of another dance reach our ears. A murmur here, a quiver in a smile there. Beneath the garlands and the songs, cracks whisper their presence.

A mischievous cousin with an overheard word, an elder aunt whose eyes dissect more than appearances, and the weight of ancestral pride that both Aarav and Meera now carry upon their young shoulders.

A fleeting moment, and suddenly Meera's eyes, those twin pools of emotion, cloud over. A word said in jest by Aarav's kin had found its mark. Her spirit, until now fluttering like a joyous bird, contracts.

As the night stretches her dark cloak over the fort, what was to be a celebration morphs into a delicate ballet of words unsaid, glances that speak volumes, and a turbulence that threatens to seep through the bejewelled splendour.

Through the corridors where once queens tread softly, Meera walks – a queen herself, but with a crown heavier than she ever imagined.

In the embrace of the fort, where countless tales of valour and love have been etched into its walls, Aarav and Meera stand as living symbols of an age-old tradition. They are at once regal in their attire, and vulnerable in their humanity. The conflict, so far a whisper, now dances like the fire before them – illuminating, and casting shadows.

It is here that we must pause and reflect upon the very nature of this conflict. Is it simply the result of a jest gone awry, or is it a representation of something far more profound? For beneath the auspices of tradition, the spirits of Aarav and Meera are bound not only to each other but to the legacies they carry, the weight of which presses upon them like the summer heat upon the golden sands.

In the silent exchanges between Meera and Aarav, there is a labyrinth of questions – the dreams they hold dear, the roles they are to assume, and the paths they are yet to walk.

From these two tales, we realize that conflicts, like delicate threads, are woven into the fabric of our relationships. They are as varied as the monsoon rains that sweep across the Indian landscape – sometimes a gentle drizzle that caresses the earth, at other times a tempest that threatens to uproot the very trees. Each conflict, a reflection of our hopes, dreams, fears, and insecurities.

But what, one must ask, is the essence that we distil from these tales? Is it the tumultuous nature of conflicts, or is it the mirror that they hold up to our souls? Perhaps it is an invitation – an invitation to delve into the layers, to listen to the whispers of the unspoken, and to embrace the beauty and pain in equal measure.

CHAPTER 3

The Unseen Threads in Personal Stories

"Friends show their love in times of trouble, not in happiness."

– Euripides

Let us now wander now into the rooms of a house that stands at the bend of a narrow lane. Through the open window, wafts of laughter, and the aroma of spices kiss the air. This house, with its worn walls and warm embraces, is a microcosm of the bonds that shape and define us.

Conflict in a family

Imagine a kitchen bathed in the golden hue of morning light. Here, a grandmother, her silver hair a crown of wisdom, weaves tales as deftly as she kneads dough. Her stories are heirlooms, and through them, the spirits of bygone generations live on.

But, there's a gentle rumble – a storm brewing with the softness of cat's paws. Across the table, with a furrowed brow, sits Ravi – a young man of the new age, armed with questions and fueled by a desire for reason. His questions, innocent as the morning dew, hold the might of tectonic plates.

Ravi, with his wide eyes that absorb the world and his mind that thirsts for the torrents of knowledge, represents the dawn of a new generation. His heart is an open book, but his roots run deep into the soil of traditions.

On one ordinary morning, as the steam rises from a cup of chai, Ravi finds himself caught in the crosswinds of change. The grandmother, whose tales he could listen to for hours, begins to recount the story of a custom in their family. A ritual that has passed down through generations but wears the weight of patriarchy. A ritual that the women of the house have complied with for as long as anyone can remember.

His heart heavy, Ravi gazes into his grandmother's eyes and poses the question – why? Why do we continue a tradition that seems to be steeped in inequality?

His grandmother's eyes, windows into a world that has seen much, cloud over. She begins to speak of times when women had little voice and how traditions, though sometimes chains, were also the threads that held the fabric of families together.

Ravi's conflict is one of values. The values that have raised him, against the values that define him. He wonders how he can honour the past, without compromising on the future.

Just as Ravi gazes into his grandmother's eyes, grappling with the weight of a tradition steeped in inequality, there echoes the age-old dilemma faced by Arjuna on the battlefield of Kurukshetra. He stands there, his hands trembling, staring into the eyes of the very people who helped shape him — his teachers, his cousins, his family. The earth beneath his feet feels like quicksand, pulling him into an abyss of moral and emotional complexity. The arrows in his quiver are not just instruments of war; they are questions aimed at the heart of what family means, and what one owes to those with whom they share blood.

With Krishna, his charioteer and guide, beside him, Arjuna is caught in the grip of an existential crisis. The battle horn has sounded, but his heartbeats drown out the noise. Krishna, sensing Arjuna's reluctance, doesn't offer simple platitudes. Instead, he opens up a vast landscape of spiritual, ethical, and moral frameworks, encouraging Arjuna to examine his role not just as a warrior, but as a member of a family and society. The message is clear: sometimes, the path of righteousness demands that we confront the most uncomfortable truths, even if that means raising our bows against those we hold dear.

Arjuna's struggle embodies the quintessence of family conflict. It exposes the raw nerve of the values that have raised him, against the values that define him. Like Arjuna, each one of us may come to a point where we must draw our proverbial bows, not in battle but in standing up for what we believe is just. It's in that pause, that moment of existential stillness, that we must make our choice — a choice that will define not just who we are, but who we become. For Arjuna, the answer lay in embracing a path that honored both his duty as a warrior and his love for his family, however agonizing the decision was.

In the simple kitchen where Ravi's dilemma unfurls, or in the grand battlefield of Kurukshetra, the essence remains the same: Tradition meets Evolution. And it's in that meeting, that clash, that intersection, that we find our most authentic selves.

Within the sanctuary of family, expectations and roles are often like the warp and weft that weave together to create the fabric of relationships. However, as individuals grow and evolve, their sense of self and aspirations might diverge from traditional familial roles, and this divergence becomes the breeding ground for conflicts.

Family roles have been passed down through generations. They are often deeply entrenched, and members are expected to conform to traditional roles based on gender, birth order, or cultural norms. These roles may include the nurturing mother, the providing father, the responsible eldest child, or the peacemaker among siblings. While these roles can provide structure and stability, they can also become restrictive moulds that stifle individuality.

As individuals, people have an intrinsic need to express their true selves. When the pursuit of one's passions, interests, or lifestyle choices clashes with family expectations, conflict arises. For instance, a parent may have a certain career in mind for their child, but the child may aspire to a completely different path. Similarly, a stay-at-home mother might wish to pursue a career, which could be met with resistance from family members accustomed to traditional gender roles.

Moreover, family roles can also come with the burden of expectations. The pressure to succeed, to uphold family honour, or to sacrifice one's desires for the sake of family can be overwhelming. This pressure often breeds resentment and frustration, leading to conflicts within the family.

An essential aspect of dealing with family conflicts is recognizing the importance of individual growth and the evolution of family dynamics. It is imperative for family members to communicate openly and to be willing to renegotiate roles and expectations. This involves recognizing and validating each member's individuality, dreams, and aspirations.

The acknowledgement of the need for change and flexibility within family roles can lead to healthier, more supportive environments. When families can navigate conflicts with openness, empathy, and mutual respect, they build relationships that are not just bound by blood but also by a shared commitment to each other's well-being and happiness. Through embracing individuality within the family unit, the fabric of family relationships becomes not just strong, but also adaptive and enriched.

It is important to recognize that sometimes the seeds of conflict in family relationships are sown by the unspoken. The silence that envelops certain topics, the unwillingness to venture into what is considered taboo or uncomfortable, creates a vacuum. In this vacuum, assumptions and misunderstandings often fester.

Family members might harbour expectations not just of roles, but also of emotional obligations. Sometimes, without voicing it, parents might expect unyielding loyalty and support, while children might long for more acceptance and less judgment. These unvoiced desires, when unmet, lead to feelings of betrayal, abandonment, or lack of love.

Conflict in families, however, is not an end unto itself. It is, in essence, a doorway. It is an opening into deeper understandings, a passage through which a family can travel to emerge into a space of greater connectivity.

When conflicts arise, it is a sign that something in the family dynamic is shifting. It is an opportunity for growth, for evolution. It's a chance to re-examine and to rebuild.

To navigate through conflicts in family relationships, it is crucial to cultivate open channels of communication. This may mean creating a safe space where each member can express their concerns without fear of judgment or retribution. It also means actively listening and trying to understand the perspectives and emotions of others.

Compromise is another cornerstone in resolving familial conflicts. There must be a recognition that for the family unit to thrive, sometimes concessions and adjustments are necessary. This doesn't mean suppressing one's desires but finding a middle ground where the core values and needs of all members are respected.

Additionally, empathy plays an enormous role. Putting oneself in another family member's shoes, and understanding their history, their fears, and their dreams, can paint the conflict in different shades. It is often in understanding that the paths to resolution are uncovered.

It's also important to remember that relationships within a family are an ongoing journey. There are no perfect solutions, and resolving conflicts doesn't mean the emergence of an idyllic state. It means forging a family dynamic that is resilient, that can withstand the winds of change, and that can grow together through the thorns and the blooms.

Ultimately, conflicts within a family are not just inevitable; they are necessary. They are the catalysts for change, the signals for the need for deeper understanding, and the stepping stones towards a family tapestry that, with its creases and mends, is richer and more beautiful.

Conflict in a Friendship

In the fragrant atmosphere of the café, Meena and Isha find solace. Their laughter usually dances through the air, and their stories form tapestries that could rival the greatest epics. Friends since childhood, they are the keepers of each other's secrets, sharing a bond that feels eternal.

This particular evening, as the sun casts its embrace through the windows, Isha's eyes are shadowed with an unspoken burden. The smile that always reaches her eyes is a mere guest on her lips today.

Meena, with her heart woven into Isha's, senses the waves of unease and gently inquires. A deep breath, and the floodgates open.

Isha shares her family's struggle. Her younger brother, always the golden child, has fallen into the clutches of addiction. The family, bound by their honour in the community, is desperately trying to hide and resolve this issue in secrecy.

Meena, her heart aching for her friend, impulsively suggests involving counsellors and reaching out to support groups. She speaks of the importance of openness and mental health.

But, as her words float through the air, she sees Isha's face harden. Isha's eyes, usually the cradle of warmth, are now clouded with the storm of unspoken words. "You don't understand. It's not that simple," she whispers, her voice strained.

The ensuing silence is an unfamiliar visitor between them.

For Meena, the path is clear – it is one of openness and seeking help. But, for Isha, the traditions of her family, their standing in the community, and the bonds that tie them to their ancestors are not so easily set aside.

Why does conflict seep into the cracks of these relationships, like monsoon waters flowing into parched earth? Could it be that in personal relationships, the ties that bind are so intricately woven with our core, that even the slightest tug feels like a quake of the soul?

Friendships, the chosen bonds, are often seen as sanctuaries where kindred spirits find solace and joy. These relationships are marked by a sense of voluntary connection – a special kind of magic, where the heart finds echoes of itself in another. In friendships, people often walk parallel paths, sharing dreams, and adventures, and shaping each other's stories.

However, just as rivers that originate from the same source can diverge into different courses, friendships too are not immune to divergence. As lives evolve, choices and paths that were once in unison might begin to diverge. When this happens, the placid waters of friendship often give way to the turbulent currents of conflict.

Such divergence can be subtle. A friend who was always the partner in crime on adventures may slowly find solace in quieter pursuits. Another, whose dreams were once aligned with yours, might discover a calling that takes them to far-off lands. These changes are but the natural courses of life's rivers, but they often unmoor the boats of friendship.

In friendships, there is often an unspoken expectation of loyalty, a belief that the choices of the other will reflect or complement one's own. When a friend makes a choice that is incongruent with these expectations, it can be seen as a betrayal or abandonment.

One must recognize that friendships, like all relationships, must breathe. They must have the space to allow each individual to grow, to explore, and sometimes to change course. Here, communication becomes a lifeline. In the throes of conflict, it is vital to express one's feelings, to voice the hurt, but also to listen. To understand that the divergence is not a diminishing of the bond, but an evolution.

In navigating conflicts in friendships, it is also essential to evaluate the nature of the bond. Are the roots deep, enriched by time and trust? Or is it a bond that, while sweet, might have run its natural course? Not all friendships are meant to be eternal, and sometimes the kindest thing is to let go.

For those bonds that are deep, resolving conflict often involves recalibration. It means finding new common ground, and building bridges that acknowledge the changes, but also celebrate the core connection that remains.

Ultimately, the value of conflict in friendships lies in the depth it can bring. In navigating the stormy waters, the bond can either find new shores or lovingly release each other to explore different horizons.

Moreover, it is essential to recognize that friendships are not stagnant pools; they are dynamic and ever-changing. Through the course of a friendship, individuals grow, and their priorities shift. The value in these conflicts is in recognizing and honouring this personal growth.

There is an inherent beauty in acknowledging the change within and in a friend. When conflicts arise, they serve as an opportunity to pause and reflect. It's a time to ask, "What is this conflict teaching me about myself, about my friend, and about the nature of our relationship?"

In some cases, this reflection can lead to a deeper understanding of each other's evolving identities. Friends may find that their bond has grown into something more mature and perhaps more profound than what they initially shared.

In other instances, the conflicts may serve as a mirror, reflecting that the friendship has reached its natural conclusion. And there's a gentle grace in acknowledging that sometimes, the most loving act is to let go.

However, not all stories of friendship tarnished by conflict find redemption or renewed understanding. Sometimes, conflict doesn't just teach; it reveals an undeniable truth—the end of a friendship's natural lifespan. The story of Mary McCarthy and Lillian Hellman, two iconic American intellectuals, eloquently attests to this sobering reality.

Both women were luminaries in their own right—Mary McCarthy, a novelist and critic, was a fearless voice of her era, while Lillian Hellman was an accomplished playwright whose works grappled with complex moral and social themes. Their friendship blossomed in intellectual salons and was nurtured over the years. Their companionship was more than casual; it was an invigorating mental repartee, a symposium of two brilliant minds.

In the early years, their ideological perspectives and aesthetic judgments seemed aligned. They found solace in each other's wit, each other's fierce intellect, and the relentless drive each had for their craft. Here were two women who could spar and debate, who could challenge and affirm each other in equal measure. Their friendship was celebrated, seen as an epitome of what intellectual camaraderie could be in an era fraught with societal prejudices and political divisions.

However, as the years unfurled, a slow corrosion began. McCarthy, a vocal critic of communism, found herself at odds with Hellman, who was known for her left-leaning views. Their political and ethical landscapes, once a backdrop to their friendship, became the very rift that divided them.

Then came the point of no return. During a televised interview, McCarthy openly criticized Hellman's integrity, stating that "every word she writes is a lie, including 'and' and 'the.'" The response from Hellman was immediate and severe, leading to a legal showdown that was as public as it was acrimonious. This was no longer a friendly disagreement; this was a fracturing, a sharp, irreversible divergence.

Their ideological differences had moved from being an intriguing layer of their friendship to becoming an insurmountable barrier. The debates that once enriched became battles that impoverished their intellectual exchange.

The conflict did not deepen their understanding of each other but instead illuminated the irreconcilable differences that lay beneath the surface of their relationship all along. It was as though a mirror had been held up to their friendship, revealing not just cracks but chasms.

The sad denouement of their relationship serves as a cautionary tale. It shows that even friendships built on intellectual rigor and mutual admiration can falter and fail when faced with profound ideological dissonance. In this tale, there's a stark lesson: sometimes the most graceful act, the final act of friendship, is to acknowledge that the journey together has reached its terminal point. To accept this is not a failure but an act of respect—for oneself, for the other, and for the history that once bound two souls.

Friendships are like vibrant threads woven into the tapestry of life. Conflicts, like knots, have the power to strengthen the fabric or indicate the need to delicately untangle and let the threads create their own intricate patterns.

It's crucial to approach conflicts in friendships with an open heart and an open mind. To realize that these conflicts are not necessarily battles to be won but conversations to be had. Through these conversations, individuals forge deeper connections with themselves and others or find the wisdom and courage to chart new waters.

As individuals tread on the paths of their journeys, they should look at conflicts in friendships as navigational aids. They are the compasses that guide and inform the heart. They hold within them lessons and opportunities that, if approached with empathy, honesty, and respect, have the power to enrich the human experience.

Conflicts in personal relationships often serve as mirrors reflecting our truest selves. They show us our strengths – our capacity for forgiveness, understanding, and love. They also unveil our limitations – our egos, our fears, and our insecurities.

But the beauty lies not just in understanding oneself but also in discovering the depth of another soul. It is in realizing that the people we share our lives with are not just roles (mother, father, friend) but are individuals with their journeys and stories.

Through conflict, we learn the art of balance; we learn when to hold on and when to let go. We learn the value of silence and the power of words. We understand the beauty of compromise and the strength in standing one's ground.

The value of conflict, therefore, lies in growth – as individuals and as companions in this journey of life. It's about painting the canvas of our relationships not just with broad strokes of joy but with intricate lines of pain, understanding, forgiveness, and love.

CHAPTER 4

Diving into the Professional World's Potpourri of Conflicts

"Success usually comes to those who are too busy to be looking for it."

– Henry David Thoreau

The Corporate Stage: Setting the Scene of a World Where Ambitions Meet and Clash

Envision a vibrant theatre where heavy, crimson curtains ascend, unveiling an ever-changing set. It throbs with the energy of countless hearts, each rhythm distinctive yet harmonizing in a symphony. This grand spectacle is the corporate realm, a stage where ambitions cloak themselves as costumes and each dawn inaugurates a fresh act imbued with promise.

In the labyrinthine halls of glass and steel, one can almost hear the whispered dreams, yearning for recognition, jostling with time-worn paths to success. The young prodigy, straight out of college, brushes shoulders with the stalwart who has been witness to the passage of countless seasons.

Each individual is a character in this play, defined by their dreams, the depth of their determination, and the hues of their hopes. Yet, where dreams dare to soar, so do clashes thunder. The cacophony can sometimes dim the brightest spirits. The fresh, idealistic mind may challenge the entrenched ways, and a cascade of chords and discords ensues. The corporate stage is set, not just for success but also for the whispers and the storms of clashing ambitions.

Office Politics: The Unwritten Rules of Power and Influence

As the lights dim and we peer closer, another layer of the corporate tapestry unveils itself – the shadow play of office politics. Here, where the coffee brews and whispers simmer, alliances are formed in the hushed tones of the pantry.

Office politics, the unwritten rules of the kingdom, can sway destinies. They are the undertows that can shape or erode paths. In the hands of the adept, they are the invisible threads that weave through the corridors of power. With a gentle tug here or a calculated word there, they can align the stars or summon the tempests.

However, it is not a realm devoid of nobility. In these shadowed alcoves, mentors are born, as are champions for change. The same politics that can manipulate can also protect and foster. They are, as in the tales of old, a double-edged sword – they can be the guardians of treasured values or the harbinger of internal strife.

As we traverse the topic of corporate politics, it becomes evident that the line between allies and adversaries can be whisper-thin. The tale of Steve Jobs and John Sculley at Apple Inc. serves as a parable in this regard. It's as if the curtain rises on a story that begins with aspirations and mentorship but culminates in a Shakespearean power struggle.

The prologue of this tale is laden with aspirations. Steve Jobs, co-founder of Apple, was a visionary by all accounts—a maestro wielding the baton of innovation. Yet, for all his technical prowess, Jobs understood the need for a seasoned hand to guide Apple through the labyrinthine world of corporate governance. Enter John Sculley, then-President of PepsiCo, whose reputation for corporate acumen promised the perfect counterbalance to Jobs' freewheeling creativity. Jobs extended an offer wrapped in eloquence and ambition: "Do you want to sell sugar water for the rest of your life, or do you want to come with me and change the world?"

Sculley took the leap, lured not just by the audacity of Jobs' vision but also by the allure of shaping history. They began as allies, complementing each other—Jobs as the dreamer, Sculley as the executor. It was a partnership that held the promise of cosmic alignments, each man fulfilling roles that seemed to complete a shared, intricate tapestry.

However, as acts passed in this opera, ideological discords started to surface. Jobs, ever the maverick, championed pioneering technologies and design philosophies that he believed would revolutionize personal computing. Sculley, in contrast, played the cautious maestro, focused on the current financial performance, market strategies, and appeasing board members who held the keys to Apple's vault. The fissure between them grew with each executive meeting, each product launch, each quarterly report. The harmony that once defined their relationship unraveled into a cacophony of divergent visions.

Until, inevitably, the rift became a chasm too deep to bridge. Sculley found himself in the curious position of having transitioned from Jobs' mentor to his most potent rival within the very empire they had both aimed to elevate. Boardroom meetings transformed into battlegrounds, agendas into weapons, and words into daggers. The climax came as expected but was shocking nonetheless: Jobs, the prodigal son of Apple, was ousted from his kingdom.

This episode does more than serve as a cautionary tale; it functions as an allegorical exposition on the precarious, often volatile, nature of power dynamics in the corporate sphere. It demonstrates that in a theater where every player is both a puppet and a puppeteer, alliances can disintegrate as swiftly as they were formed. The story of Jobs and Sculley resonates as a classic example of how high the stakes can be when navigating the intricate ballet of ambitions, aspirations, and unwritten rules within the corporate world.

As we journey through the hallowed halls of the corporate world, we must recognize and understand the nature of these unwritten rules. The corridors whisper the secrets to those who listen – the secrets of not just surviving but flourishing in the tapestry where power and influence dance their eternal waltz.

Diversity in Ambitions: The Mosaic of Aspirations in the Workplace

In the corporate world, the threads of individual ambitions create a rich mosaic. The young intern dreams of revolutionizing the industry, the seasoned executive eyes the corner office as the summit of their lifelong climb, and the diligent assistant seeks recognition and a voice in the throng. Each thread is vital, adding depth and texture to the larger picture.

However, the kaleidoscope of ambitions can sometimes jostle for space and light. When the lens through which we view our aspirations becomes myopic, the mosaic may blur into a cacophony. It is crucial to recognize and respect the diversity in ambitions. Each aspiration has a place under the sun, and the tapestry is all the richer for it.

As our journey continues through the corporate landscape, we find ourselves entangled in a web – a web woven by words, expressions, and silences. Communication, the lifeline of human interaction, can sometimes become a twisted labyrinth in the workplace.

A casual remark, a joke shared between cubicles, or even the silence in a meeting room – these can become the triggers for discord. In the world of instant messaging and emails, the absence of context and the human touch can sometimes render words sterile or laden with unintended meaning.

It is in these moments that the wisdom of choosing words with care and discerning the waves beneath the surface become invaluable. Communication can build bridges or create chasms – navigating this realm demands not just skill, but empathy.

Navigating Hierarchies: The Delicate Dance of Climbing the Corporate Ladder

As one ventures into the professional realm, navigating hierarchies becomes an integral part of the journey. The corporate ladder, with its many tiers, represents the structure and chain of command within an organization. Climbing this ladder is often equated with professional success, but it's important to recognize that with each step upward, the challenges and responsibilities multiply.

- **Understanding the Complexity:**

  Climbing the corporate ladder is not merely about bagging promotions; it's about navigating a complex environment where decision-making, leadership skills, and adaptability play a vital role. Each level of hierarchy brings with it an array of stakeholders whose interests, expectations, and perspectives vary.

- **Balancing Leadership:**

  As individuals move up, they transition from being team members to taking on leadership roles. This necessitates a balance between delegation and taking charge, between listening and directing. The weight of decisions grows heavier as their impact broadens. Here, leadership is as much about guiding others as it is about continuous self-improvement.

- **Building Networks:**

  Relationships within the corporate environment are crucial. As one climbs the corporate ladder, the ability to forge alliances and networks becomes indispensable. Knowing who to approach for what information, understanding the informal power structures, and building rapport with colleagues and subordinates are essential skills.

- **Handling Increased Visibility:**

  As one ascends the hierarchy, visibility increases. Actions and decisions are more scrutinized, and there is less room for error. Being in a higher position often means being in the spotlight, and the ability to handle pressure and scrutiny is key.

- **Dealing with Trade-offs:**

  Moving up often comes with trade-offs. This could mean longer hours, less time for personal life, and sometimes, grappling with ethical dilemmas. A higher position might necessitate difficult choices, and it is important to be prepared to face them.

- **Staying Grounded:**

  It's easy to lose touch with one's roots when climbing the corporate ladder. However, staying grounded and remembering the values and principles that shaped one's early career can be pivotal. This not only helps in making well-rounded decisions but also in earning the respect and trust of peers and subordinates.

A Glimpse Into How Conflict Could Manifest Within A Corporate Environment

The Reluctant Entrepreneur: From Cubicle to Corner Office

Our tale brings us to the life of Aditi, a talented software engineer in one of the leading IT firms in Hyderabad, India. A person of few words, Aditi's world was composed of lines of code that spoke more to her than any human language. She cherished the predictability of her cubicle and thrived in the structured environment that her corporate job provided.

One fine day, the tranquility of Aditi's life was shattered. A new project manager, Ramesh, took charge, and he brought with him a whirlwind of change. His unconventional approach towards work and his incessant demand for 'thinking outside the box' clashed with Aditi's way of functioning. This divergence soon turned into an open conflict when Ramesh publicly criticized Aditi's work during a team meeting.

Humiliated and dejected, Aditi seriously considered leaving the job she loved. However, in the depths of despair, she began to see the situation in a different light. She recognized that her conflict with Ramesh was not just about differing working styles but about her own resistance to change and experimentation.

This realization was a turning point. Aditi began to dabble in side projects where she could exercise more creativity. What began as a coping mechanism soon turned into a passion as she discovered a world beyond her cubicle. She started participating in hackathons, collaborated with other engineers, and even developed a prototype for an application that aimed at bridging communication gaps in the corporate world.

Six months down the line, at another of the numerous corporate meetings, Aditi did the unthinkable. She tendered her resignation. But this was no ordinary exit. Aditi left to start her own venture based on the prototype she developed. The reluctant entrepreneur was born out of the ashes of conflict.

As years rolled on, Aditi's start-up grew in leaps and bounds. The young woman, who once found solace in the predictability of a cubicle, now helmed an innovative company from her corner office.

Aditi's story stands as a testament to the transformative power of conflict. In the corporate battlefield, where swords of ambition and shields of caution often clash, her journey reminds us that sometimes conflict can be the spark that lights the path of innovation, turning the reluctant into the triumphant.

Let's envision the same scenario with a different perspective and examine the devastating impact of conflict:

Let us reimagine Aditi's story through a different lens.

In this alternative scenario, when Ramesh steps in as the new project manager with his unconventional methods, the conflict between his approach and Aditi's established routines intensifies. Instead of the conflict being a catalyst for growth, it festers and creates a toxic atmosphere. Communication breaks down, and Aditi starts feeling alienated and unappreciated.

Aditi's resentment grows, and rather than seeking ways to adapt or understand Ramesh's perspective, she becomes entrenched in her position. She begins to see Ramesh not as a colleague with different methods but as an adversary intent on undermining her.

On the other side, Ramesh, instead of trying to bridge the gap, becomes increasingly impatient with Aditi's resistance to his ideas. He begins to marginalize her, and the team begins to take sides, polarizing the entire department.

As this conflict escalates, the productivity of the team diminishes. The creativity and collaboration that once thrived start to wane as the focus shifts from collective goals to personal vendettas.

Aditi, feeling cornered, decides to leave the company. However, the conflict has taken a toll on her. Her confidence is shaken, and she questions her own abilities and worth. Instead of the entrepreneurial venture, which was a possibility in the positive scenario, Aditi now hesitates to take risks. The shadow of the conflict looms large, stifling her potential.

In this version of Aditi's story, we see the destructive power of conflict. The same elements that, under different circumstances, could have led to growth and evolution, here lead to alienation, loss of potential, and the weakening of the team's fabric.

This demonstrates that conflict, much like fire, can either forge stronger metal or consume everything in its path. The outcome depends on how the individuals involved, as well as the organization, manage and navigate through the conflict. It's a reminder that awareness, communication, empathy, and the willingness to adapt are crucial in determining whether conflict becomes a tool for growth or a weapon of destruction.

The Alchemy of Conflict in the Corporate Cauldron

In the molten core of the corporate world, conflicts churn and bubble, mixing and reacting to create an alchemy that can change the very essence of organizations and individuals. It is through this alchemy that the static evolves, and the monotonous turns vibrant.

Transformation: The Spark that Ignites Change

In the first version of Aditi's story, conflict acts as a powerful catalyst for transformation. When Ramesh, the new project manager, introduces unconventional approaches that clash with Aditi's established ways, tension ensues. However, in this scenario, Aditi embraces the conflict as an opportunity for self-reflection and growth.

She begins by communicating her concerns with Ramesh and actively listening to his perspective. Through open dialogue, they find common ground and combine the strengths of both their approaches. This collaboration leads to innovative solutions that benefit the team and the organization.

Aditi's willingness to adapt is fundamental to this transformation. The conflict pushes her out of her comfort zone, forcing her to reevaluate her methods and beliefs. This personal evolution eventually leads Aditi to explore her entrepreneurial aspirations and launch her own venture. Here, conflict is the spark that ignites change, leading to personal and professional transformation.

Destruction: The Consuming Flames of Unmanaged Conflict

Conversely, in the second version of Aditi's story, the very same conflict takes a destructive turn. The initial friction between Aditi and Ramesh turns into a full-blown blaze as neither party is willing to communicate or compromise. The conflict escalates, consuming not only their working relationship but also affecting the entire team.

Aditi becomes entrenched in her position, perceiving Ramesh's methods as a personal affront. In turn, Ramesh marginalizes her, causing further polarization within the team. Productivity and collaboration take a backseat as the focus shifts to protecting personal turf.

Ultimately, the unmanaged conflict leads to Aditi's departure from the company. However, the experience leaves her burnt out and doubting her abilities, preventing her from realizing her potential. The conflict, instead of being a catalyst for growth, becomes a wildfire that scorches everything in its path.

These contrasting versions of Aditi's story underscore the potent dual nature of conflict in the corporate world. They remind us that conflict is an inevitable part of the dynamic professional landscape, but its outcomes are malleable. The alchemy of conflict can lead to transformation or destruction, depending on how it is managed, communicated, and perceived.

The Price and Reward: Balancing Personal Costs with Professional Gains

Conflicts within the corporate setting often present a complex equation where personal costs and professional gains need to be balanced. Navigating conflicts effectively requires understanding the nuances of this balance and making choices that reflect not only professional aspirations but also personal well-being.

For instance, an individual who relentlessly pursues professional advancement at the cost of personal relationships and health may attain coveted positions but may find the victory hollow and isolating. Conversely, avoiding all conflicts to maintain personal peace may lead to stagnation and missed opportunities for growth.

The balance lies in discernment – the ability to gauge which conflicts are worth engaging in and which are better left unaddressed. It's about identifying the battles that align with one's values and long-term goals and recognizing the personal resources required in terms of time, energy, and emotional capital.

Making conscious decisions, considering the personal costs and the potential professional gains, and being mindful of one's values and boundaries, helps individuals navigate conflicts without compromising their integrity or well-being.

The Cauldron's Secret Recipe: Turning Conflicts into Opportunities for Growth and Collaboration

The secret recipe for turning conflicts into opportunities lies in perspective and approach. The very nature of conflict means there is a divergence in views, which, if harnessed effectively, can lead to creativity, innovation, and collaboration. Below are the essential ingredients for this secret recipe:

- **Embrace Diversity of Thought:** Understand that diversity in viewpoints can be an asset. Different perspectives can complement each other and contribute to a more comprehensive understanding of issues.
- **Effective Communication:** Master the art of communication. Express your thoughts clearly and, more importantly, listen to understand. Encourage open dialogue where team members feel safe to share their opinions.
- **Empathy and Respect:** Place yourself in the shoes of others and try to understand their perspectives and motivations. Displaying empathy can de-escalate conflicts and open the door to collaboration.
- **Focus on Common Goals:** Identifying and concentrating on common objectives can create a sense of unity. Use the shared goals as a foundation to explore various paths and solutions.

- **Flexibility and Adaptability:** Be open to change and willing to adapt your methods and approaches. Flexibility is key to finding middle ground and creating innovative solutions.
- **Reflection and Learning:** After a conflict has been addressed, take time to reflect on the process and outcomes. What can be learned? What could have been done differently? Use this insight for future conflicts.

By incorporating these ingredients into the corporate cauldron, conflicts can be transformed into powerful forces for growth, innovation, and collaboration. The alchemy of conflict is a potent tool, and with the right ingredients and careful handling, it can change base metals into gold.

CHAPTER 5

Delving Into the Intricacies of Romantic Conflicts: Examining Their Origins and Progression

"The course of true love never did run smooth."

– **William Shakespeare**

Romance, a dance of hearts, often finds itself entwined with threads of discord. The melody of love occasionally strikes a dissonant chord, introducing a new rhythm, an offbeat note, yet a vivid reminder of our multifaceted humanity. What stirs this discord, and how does it modulate the symphony of love?

The causes of conflict in romantic relationships are as diverse as the symphony's many notes. Divergent dreams playing offbeat, clashing communication styles disrupting the harmony, fiscal frictions creating an unwanted crescendo, or the simple discord of habits – these are but a few notes that can disrupt the melody of love. Like misinterpreted lyrics in a song, these disagreements can cause an unsettling resonance, setting the stage for the symphony of conflict.

These disruptive melodies, though often uncomfortable, leave a powerful imprint. Communication may falter, like an out-of-tune instrument, leading to a dissonant performance filled with frustration and missed cues. Emotional bonds might fray, transforming a harmonious duet into a disjoined solo act. Empathy may wane, as each musician becomes engrossed in their solo, losing sight of the orchestra's collective rhythm.

Romantic relationships are a complex landscape, where conflicts emerge in various forms, each with its distinct dynamics. Let's explore some of the most prevalent ones:

Financial Conflicts: Financial conflicts, as with many disagreements, start as small seeds. A seemingly insignificant argument over an extravagant purchase or a casual comment about a partner's financial habits might be the genesis. But, as these disagreements remain unresolved, they take root, growing into a tree that casts a shadow over the relationship.

In a world where money is not just a medium of exchange but a symbol of power, status, and freedom, how a person manages their finances is a direct reflection of their values and priorities. One person's prudent saving could be perceived as miserly control by the other. Conversely, one's spontaneous spending could be seen as a carefree enjoyment of life or an irresponsible disregard for future stability.

These financial disagreements often bring to the surface deep-seated beliefs about money ingrained since childhood. A person who grew up in a household where money was always tight might be more inclined towards frugality and saving for a rainy day. On the other hand, someone who experienced a financially secure upbringing might see money as a means for enjoyment and lifestyle enhancement.

The conflict intensifies when these differences in financial attitudes intersect with the shared responsibilities and collective decision-making inherent in a relationship. The stage is thus set for conflict, where money becomes not just a tool for transaction but a weapon in a power struggle.

In these financial disagreements, what's at stake isn't just the state of the joint bank account, but the understanding, respect, and compromise needed for a shared life.

The turbulence can cause strain and resentment, challenging the couple to look beyond the numbers and navigate the complicated map of financial harmony.

Antony and Cleopatra: The Confluence of Love, Power, and Finance

Though their tale is set in an era far removed from modern complexities, the love story of Mark Antony and Cleopatra is not without its financial tensions. Antony was a Roman general with obligations and ambitions in Rome, while Cleopatra was the Queen of Egypt, one of the wealthiest kingdoms of the time. Their alliance was as much about love as it was about political and financial gains.

In the embrace of Cleopatra's affluence, Antony found not just love but also a lifestyle that distanced him from the austere Roman ideals of temperance and moderation. The Egyptian court was a locus of abundance—extravagant feasts, immense wealth, and the allure of luxury that Rome, for all its power, could scarcely rival. This wasn't just a choice of environment; it became a question of identity. Antony's Roman contemporaries saw him not as a man intoxicated by love, but as one compromised by the mire of Egyptian extravagance. He became the protagonist in a Roman tragedy, a cautionary figure ensnared by wealth and seduced away from duty.

For Cleopatra, the stakes were no less significant. Her relationship with Antony was a political calculation wrapped in the silks of romance. Egypt needed Rome as much as Rome needed Egypt; the relationship assured a military alliance that fortified her reign. However, her fortune and kingdom were not just enticements but bargaining chips. Antony received financial and military aid, but he also conferred upon Cleopatra titles and territories that expanded her realm and solidified her power. Money wasn't just an accessory to their relationship; it was its underpinning, a silent partner in their romantic venture.

When the alliances shifted and their stars crossed, the sword of Damocles finally fell. Their tale spiraled into a tragedy, immortalized in Shakespearean prose, and became a parable on the perils of mingling financial dependencies with romantic yearnings. Antony and Cleopatra's epic serves as an indelible reminder that financial conflict in a relationship often emerges as a manifestation of an underlying struggle for power, influence, and identity.

In a tale as grand as theirs, what strikes most is the inescapable truth that when romantic love is woven with financial interests, the tapestry becomes far more intricate and perilous. Here, money transcended its role as a mere tool or asset; it became a dynamic entity, fraught with its own emotional and psychological weight. When financial complexities emerge in the landscape of love, they become not just a question of fiscal management but a turbulent vortex, revealing deeper dimensions of the relationship that demand understanding and, above all, negotiation.

The saga of Antony and Cleopatra could fittingly embellish this section of the chapter on financial conflicts in romantic relationships.It demonstrates how romantic entanglements can be fraught with woven emotional and financial connections, so intricately intertwined that tugging on one thread could cause everything to unravel. Their story prompts us to explore the undercurrents that money can reveal, reminding us that when financial conflict casts its shadow over love, the stakes become as monumental as the empires of old.

Communication Disparities: The dance of communication in relationships is a delicate ballet of words, silence, gestures, and emotions. It is a performance that requires attunement not just to the spoken language but to the intricate vocabulary of non-verbal cues and emotional expressiveness. When the dance is harmonious, it is a symphony of shared understanding. However, when individual communication styles clash, it transforms into a battlefield of misunderstanding and frustration.

Every person carries with them a unique communication blueprint. These patterns, etched into their psyche by their experiences, shape how they convey thoughts, feelings, and desires. When two such unique blueprints come together in a relationship, it isn't always an easy fit.

One partner may be an open book, their words and emotions flowing freely, coloring their conversation with their vibrancy. They may favor direct communication, leaving little room for ambiguity, and expect the same level of openness from their partner.

Contrastingly, the other partner may be more akin to a calm lake, their thoughts and feelings running deep beneath a serene surface. Their communication style might be more indirect or understated, leaning towards subtlety rather than overt expressiveness. They may be more comfortable expressing themselves through actions rather than words, leading to a chasm in communication.

This clash of communication styles can ignite the fuse of conflict. The expressive partner might perceive the other's reserved style as coldness or disinterest. In contrast, the reserved partner may feel overwhelmed by their partner's emotional intensity and become defensive.

Furthermore, misunderstandings can proliferate when non-verbal cues are misinterpreted. A casual, off-hand gesture or an unintended tone of voice can become the spark that lights the powder keg of conflict.

Dido and Aeneas: A Classical Drama of Missed Signals and Misinterpreted Intentions

The tale of Dido and Aeneas serves as a cautionary story that underscores the gravity of communication, or lack thereof, in shaping the destiny of romantic partnerships. Residing in the ancient text of Virgil's "Aeneid," their story reverberates through time as an exemplar of how silence and unsaid words can be as deadly as swords in the realm of love.

Dido, the revered Queen of Carthage, and Aeneas, the Trojan hero burdened by prophecy, initially seem to epitomize the romantic ideal. Their affection transcends political alliances and power dynamics, carving a private sanctuary where love reigns supreme. Yet, hovering like a dark cloud over their bliss is Aeneas's prophetic mission—a destiny foretold that entails founding Rome, the city that would one day conquer the world.

Even as Dido immerses herself in the intoxicating sensation of love, constructing in her mind a future built upon mutual affection and shared governance, Aeneas is ensnared by an internal conflict that gnaws at his conscience. His love for Dido wages a silent war against his preordained duty to his future descendants. This tension manifests as a distinct absence of open dialogue between the two lovers. Aeneas grapples silently with his dilemma, while Dido remains blissfully unaware of the monumental choice her lover faces. The tragedy lies not in their incompatible destinies, but in Aeneas's failure to communicate the depths of his conflict to Dido.

The catastrophic climax occurs when Aeneas, nudged by divine intervention, surreptitiously prepares to leave Carthage. Dido's world unravels when she discovers his imminent departure. His failure to openly discuss his departure, his prophecy, or the duty that beckons him leaves Dido feeling betrayed, culminating in a sense of despair so deep that she takes her own life. Her heart-wrenching final words encapsulate the tragic breakdown in their communication: a lament not just for lost love, but for the lost opportunity to understand and perhaps reconcile their diverging paths.

The demise of Dido serves as a poignant reminder that love alone is not the cornerstone of a sustainable relationship. Open, honest communication is the lifeblood that nourishes the heart of romance. Their story exemplifies the tragic consequences of communication disparity—a powerful example of how misunderstandings and unspoken feelings can lay waste to even the most passionate of relationships.

Thus, communication disparities present a unique challenge in relationships. The words left unsaid can become as significant as the ones spoken, and the promise of understanding can get lost in translation. As these miscommunications stack up, they construct a wall that divides the couple, leaving them longing for a bridge of understanding.

Intimacy and Sexual Conflicts: Intimacy, whether emotional or physical, is a delicate dance that partners strive to synchronize in a relationship. It's a complex composition, weaving together the subtle notes of desires, expectations, and vulnerability. Ideally, it's a symphony that seamlessly merges two individual melodies into a harmonious whole. Yet, disparities in this dance often lead to discord, breeding conflict in romantic relationships.

Intimacy, a cornerstone of romantic relationships, is much more than a physical connection. It is the ability to share one's self, in all their vulnerability, with their partner. Each partner brings their unique understanding and expectation of intimacy, influenced by their past experiences, personal values, and emotional needs. When these expectations diverge, it can feel as though they are dancing to different tunes.

One partner may equate intimacy with sharing their innermost feelings and thoughts, expecting deep emotional conversations as a path to connect. Meanwhile, the other may find intimacy in shared activities, quiet moments, or physical touch. This mismatch can result in feelings of emotional disconnection, leading to misunderstandings and resentment.

Another critical aspect of intimacy is the sexual relationship. Just like any other aspect of the relationship, sexual desires and needs vary greatly between individuals. One partner may have a higher libido, equating sexual intimacy with love and affection, while the other may seek emotional connection as a precursor to sexual intimacy. Differences in sexual desire, when unaddressed, can lead to feelings of rejection and dissatisfaction, adding fuel to the fire of conflict.

Finally, struggles with vulnerability can create a significant roadblock to intimacy. Opening oneself up to another person, revealing the raw, unguarded parts of oneself, can be a daunting task. When a partner is not able to be vulnerable, it can limit the emotional depth of the relationship, resulting in feelings of distance and loneliness.

Heloise and Abelard: When Minds and Bodies Don't Align

Within the fabric of enduring love stories, the passionate bond shared between Heloise, an intellectually gifted young woman, and Abelard, a highly esteemed scholar of his era, stands as an exemplar of the intricate interplay between intellectual and sexual intimacy. Their relationship beautifully weaves together the realms of the mind and the heart, a testament to the profound connection that exists between two souls. In 12th-century Paris, a time when women's education was often relegated to the backburner of societal priorities, Heloise's keen intellect found a *counterpart in Abelard, her tutor. Their discussions on philosophy, ethics, and theology were not merely academic exercises but an intense meeting of minds that transcended the lecture halls into the privacy of their hearts.*

But, as with any tale of great passion, there came complications. Heloise became pregnant, a circumstance that, given the social norms of the time, forced them into a secret marriage and ultimately, into the traditional roles of wife and mother for Heloise, and monk for Abelard—roles that stifled the intellectual communion they had enjoyed. Heloise was sent to a nunnery, a grim but practical solution to 'resolve' the situation, while Abelard continued his monastic life.

The story didn't end there; it was immortalized in the letters they wrote to each other later in life. Heloise's letters spoke volumes about the struggle she faced, a constant tension between her intellectual capabilities and societal expectations as a wife and mother. Abelard's replies revealed a man grappling with guilt over the course their lives had taken but also yearning for the intellectual exchange they once freely enjoyed. They wrote about theology and philosophy, yes, but their letters were also filled with a palpable longing for a connection that had been lost, demonstrating how a fulfilling relationship often rests on multiple forms of intimacy.

Indeed, navigating the landscape of intimacy and sexual conflicts is like walking a tightrope. The journey requires balance, understanding, and a shared language of love. However, when these are lacking, it can give birth to a storm of conflict, casting dark clouds over the relationship. These conflicts, although deeply personal and sensitive, are crucial conversations that need to occur for a relationship to evolve and deepen.

Parenting Styles and Family Dynamics: Navigating the waters of family life and parenting is akin to steering a ship through a labyrinth of uncharted territories. The map for this journey is often drawn from personal experiences, familial values, and individual beliefs about family and parenting. When partners hold fundamentally different maps, the journey together can become a turbulent voyage of conflict.

Parenting, a role filled with profound love and overwhelming responsibility, brings a multitude of decisions. Each decision, each rule, each value imparted, shapes a child's life in ways more profound than one can fathom. This burden of influence can become a crucible of conflict when partners have disparate views on parenting.

One partner might adhere to a more authoritative style, prioritizing discipline and structured routines, believing that this prepares children for the real world. In contrast, the other might lean towards a more permissive approach, emphasizing freedom and creativity, nurturing independence and self-expression in the child. These contrasting styles, when unable to find a middle ground, can lead to regular clashes, creating an environment of uncertainty and stress for everyone involved.

Even the philosophy on what constitutes care and love can become a battleground. Concepts of quality time, balance between work and family, views on what is essential for a child's happiness and success – all become ingredients for potential conflict.

Additionally, conflicts are not confined to the immediate family nucleus. They can radiate outwards, ensnaring the extended family. The involvement of in-laws and relatives, their influence on the family's dynamics, the respect accorded to them, and the boundaries set for their involvement are potential triggers for disputes. These conflicts can put additional strain on the couple's relationship, making the family's harmony feel like an elusive goal.

Cultural differences can further exacerbate these conflicts, especially in families that bring together diverse backgrounds. Each culture, each tradition, carries its unique set of values and norms about family life and parenting. When these differences are not acknowledged and appreciated, they can create rifts that widen over time, fueling the flame of conflict.

Anna Karenina: The Strain of Cultural Norms on Family Harmony

The Russian classic, Anna Karenina, penned by Leo Tolstoy, provides a searing lens through which we can examine the pernicious impact of societal norms on familial relationships. Anna Karenina is a woman ensnared by societal expectations. Married to Alexei Alexandrovich Karenin, a high-ranking government official, she ostensibly has everything a woman of her time could wish for: wealth, social standing, and a child. Yet, she feels emotionally stifled and detached from her spouse, a man more engrossed in his social and political obligations than in the emotional sustenance of his family.

Anna's decision to leave her husband and son in pursuit of love with Count Vronsky is not just a mere act of infidelity; it is a rebellion against the societal norms that have long confined her. She chooses emotional fulfillment over societal approval, a choice that comes at an exorbitant price. The ensuing scandal tarnishes not just Anna but her entire family, showcasing how one person's divergence from societal expectations can cast long shadows over all related family dynamics.

Interestingly, her husband Karenin is not an overtly malicious man, but his staunch adherence to societal expectations makes him indifferent to the emotional complexities that govern human relationships. He is more worried about social disgrace than he is about the shattered emotional landscape of his family. This near-mechanical compliance with cultural norms turns him into an unwitting contributor to his family's disintegration.

Therefore, Anna Karenina serves as a haunting example of how cultural norms can dictate the behavior of individuals in a family unit to the extent that they lose sight of what should be their true focus: mutual understanding, emotional support, and a harmonious coexistence. In many modern relationships, these societal pressures may manifest differently but are no less potent. Whether it's the expectation to maintain a 'perfect family image' on social media or the community pressures to prioritize certain educational or career paths for children, the erosion of family harmony in the face of societal norms remains a pressing issue.

The arena of parenting and family dynamics is a potential minefield of conflicts. But amidst these challenges, it is important to remember that these conflicts are born out of a shared love and a shared responsibility – to create a nurturing environment for a family to grow and flourish. The key is to recognize these differences and navigate them with understanding, patience, and respect.

Life Goals and Priorities: Every individual embarks on the journey of life with a unique compass – a set of personal goals, dreams, and priorities that guide their path. When two individuals unite in a romantic relationship, their paths converge. But the alignment of two unique compasses is no easy task, and therein lies a fertile ground for conflict.

Life goals and priorities form the bedrock of personal identity and purpose. They serve as the guiding stars, illuminating the path towards fulfillment and satisfaction. When partners harbor different life goals, or when their priorities are not in sync, the harmony of their shared path can be disrupted.

Consider career aspirations, for instance. One partner might dream of climbing the corporate ladder, willing to invest time and effort to reach the pinnacle of their professional life. The other partner might prioritize work-life balance, seeking a career that allows ample time for personal pursuits and family life. These divergent aspirations, if not addressed with mutual understanding and respect, can lead to a rift in the relationship. The conflict intensifies when these aspirations necessitate difficult choices, such as relocation for a job opportunity or sacrificing career progression for family life.

Another arena where differing life goals can fuel conflict is the decision about starting a family. One partner might envision a future replete with the joys and challenges of parenthood, while the other might prefer a child-free life, cherishing personal freedom and other pursuits. This divergence goes beyond a mere disagreement; it strikes at the core of personal values and visions for the future.

Even the choice of where to live – the hustle and bustle of city life or the tranquillity of the countryside, close to family or an independent life, a stationary home or a nomadic lifestyle – these are not just decisions about a physical place. They reflect deeper desires for a certain quality of life, for comfort, for community, for adventure.

These conflicts over life goals and priorities are not just about the specific disagreements that surface. They are about the struggle to align two unique paths, two distinct visions towards a shared destination. It is a balancing act of honoring individual dreams while nurturing a shared dream, a dance between personal growth and the growth of a relationship.

Zelda and F. Scott Fitzgerald: The Double-Edged Sword of Ambition

Zelda and F. Scott Fitzgerald stand as quintessential figures of the Jazz Age, a time known for its extravagant parties, bohemian lifestyle, and an ethos that celebrated unrestrained ambition. Yet, behind the glittering façade of their public life lay a mosaic of personal ambitions, dreams deferred, and conflicting priorities.

Scott's ambition was clear-cut from the outset: to become one of America's literary giants. Every party attended, every glass of champagne poured, served as fodder for his creative pursuits. His magnum opus, "The Great Gatsby," mirrored his own ambitious pursuits—just as Jay Gatsby was entranced by the green light across the bay, Scott was enticed by the allure of literary immortality.

Zelda, often reduced to the role of "the wife of F. Scott Fitzgerald," had ambitions that were no less grand but far less linear. A writer, dancer, and artist in her own right, Zelda wanted to be more than just the muse or the socialite wife; she wanted her own individual fame and recognition. While Scott sought immortality through his words, Zelda sought it through her diverse creative talents, an ambition no less valid but one that often found itself at odds with her husband's career.

Their story serves as a cautionary tale on multiple fronts. First, it exemplifies the dangers of what can happen when a couple's ambitions are in competition rather than harmony. Their passionate love for each other was often overshadowed by their individual pursuits of greatness, leading to emotional neglect and estrangement.

Secondly, their story raises the issue of financial instability as a complicating factor. Scott's extravagant lifestyle and Zelda's costly artistic pursuits put significant financial strain on their relationship, which in turn exacerbated their emotional conflicts. Money, or the lack thereof, became yet another battleground for their competing dreams.

Zelda and Scott's relationship encapsulates the intense vulnerability that comes with ambition. For all their dreams and desires, both were fraught with insecurities and fears of failure—emotions that became magnified within the confines of their relationship.

Amidst the intricate web of conflicts, it is crucial to bear in mind that these differences of opinion are not inherently synonymous with destruction.Instead, they offer opportunities for deeper understanding, for mutual respect, and for creating a shared vision that respects individual goals while forging a common path forward.

Conflicts, as challenging as they may be, serve as an illuminating mirror, revealing the undercurrents often lurking beneath the surface of romantic relationships. They throw light on the vulnerabilities, the fears, the insecurities, the strengths, and the power dynamics at play.

When we look into this mirror, we are often confronted by our true selves, by our deepest desires and our most haunting fears. We are challenged to question, to introspect, and to understand ourselves and our partners on a deeper level. This introspection, while it can be painful, holds immense power. It offers the possibility of transformation, of growth, and of deepening connection.

Charting the Path Forward

The conflicts also paint a picture of the intricate dance of power dynamics in relationships. They lay bare the delicate balance of give-and-take, of compromise and assertion, of respect and challenge. They expose the patterns that can, unconsciously, become embedded in the relationship fabric, shaping its texture and its feel.

As we navigate the tumultuous waters of conflict, the horizon of our relationship may seem obscured by darkness and uncertainty.Yet, amidst these gathering clouds, there exists a silver lining. For every conflict holds within it the seeds of resolution, the potential for growth, the promise of a more profound understanding, and the chance for a fresh start.

These conflicts, these storms, they don't just shake us; they shape us. They don't merely challenge our relationship; they offer us a chance to strengthen it, to build it on a foundation of mutual understanding, respect, and love.

Thus, as daunting as these conflicts may appear, they are not just about the clash of differing perspectives or desires. They are about the beautiful, messy, and transformative process of two individuals striving to build a shared life, preserving their unique identities while nurturing a bond that transcends the sum of its parts.

The evolution of these conflicts, the paths they carve in our shared journey, and the lessons they offer, will be the focus of our exploration as we continue our journey in the realm of romantic conflicts. We shall delve deeper into these stormy waters, guided by the beacon of understanding, navigating our way towards resolution and growth.

CHAPTER 6

The Lover's Ballad – Passion, Pain, and Reconciliation

"The emotion that can break your heart is sometimes the very one that heals it."

– Nicholas Sparks

A Love Withered

Anjali was a young woman from Mumbai who worked as a sales associate at a bustling local supermarket. Her life revolved around the cacophony of price checks and bargaining customers. Each evening, she would return home, tired but content, to her husband, Ravi.

Ravi was a taxi driver, navigating the busy streets of Mumbai with honking horns and impatient passengers. Despite the chaotic traffic and the stress, he found a strange solace behind the wheel, with the city's heartbeat pulsating around him.

They met in the most ordinary of circumstances – Anjali was his fare one rainy evening. They connected over shared dreams and mutual respect for their hard-working parents. Over time, they fell in love, got married, and shared a small but cozy apartment.

Their life together was simple, filled with laughter and shared dreams. They would save their pennies to enjoy a movie at the local cinema, and Sundays were reserved for shared homemade meals and long walks along the beach. Their love was their cocoon, their refuge.

However, as years rolled by, the cocoon began to unfurl. The laughter turned into long silences and the shared dreams into solitary thoughts. The daily grind of their jobs started to take a toll on them. They began living like two strangers under the same roof, bound by routine rather than love.

The day Anjali found a note from Ravi suggesting separation, she wasn't surprised. She had felt the distance growing, the invisible wall between them getting thicker. Yet, it was a hard blow, a cruel reminder of their failing relationship. Her heart ached, but she knew it was inevitable.

She remembered their earlier days, filled with shared dreams and laughter. Now, they were just echoes of a past they both longed for but couldn't recapture. She thought about Ravi's tired eyes, once filled with love, now reflecting exhaustion and disappointment.

Anjali realized they were just two ordinary people carrying extraordinary expectations of love and life. Their love, once vibrant and full of promise, had fallen victim to their monotonous routine. It wasn't a single moment or a dramatic argument that had brought them here, but a slow and painful withering of their bond.

Accepting the note, she agreed to Ravi's suggestion. The decision was heavy with unshed tears and unsaid words. The silence between them spoke volumes of their failed attempts to hold on to their withering relationship.

As the sun set that evening, she packed her bags. There was a strange calmness in her heart, a sense of closure. Their love story was ending, not with a bang, but a whimper.

Before leaving, she turned towards Ravi, "I guess we were like those ships passing in the night, Ravi. We saw each other, we shared our light, but then we drifted apart. It's sad, but that's life, isn't it?"

With a deep sigh, Ravi nodded, "Yes, Anjali, that's life."

The primary conflict in Anjali and Ravi's relationship was the gradual emotional disconnect that stemmed from their monotonous routine and the burdens of their everyday jobs. The early years of their marriage were full of shared dreams and mutual enjoyment of simple pleasures, which slowly faded into a mechanical routine, devoid of emotional intimacy and personal connection.

- **Lack of Communication:** Over time, they ceased to share their thoughts and dreams with each other, leading to a wide communication gap. They lived together, but their emotional worlds drifted apart, resulting in growing loneliness and alienation.
- **Monotonous Routine:** Their routine-based lives, revolving around their jobs, led to a sense of monotony that began to affect their relationship. They had little time or energy left to engage with each other emotionally, leading to a gradual disintegration of their bond.
- **Unaddressed Emotional Needs:** They ignored the emotional void growing between them, failing to address their unmet emotional needs. They became more like roommates than a married couple, leading to dissatisfaction and unhappiness.

Addressing these issues could have potentially salvaged their relationship. Here are a few measures that they could have considered:

- **Open Communication:** They should have kept the lines of communication open, discussing their feelings, fears, and dreams. Sharing thoughts and emotions can create a stronger emotional bond and prevent feelings of alienation.
- **Break the Monotony:** They could have tried to break the monotony of their lives by incorporating new experiences. These could range from exploring new hobbies, going on occasional trips, or even having a 'date night' once a week to keep the spark alive.
- **Work-Life Balance:** Prioritizing a work-life balance would have been crucial. Although work is necessary, it should not consume one's life entirely. They needed to carve out quality time for each other.
- **Seek Professional Help:** When their personal attempts at resolution seemed to fail, they could have considered seeking help from a professional counselor or a marriage therapist who could guide them through their issues and provide strategies to reconnect and rekindle their relationship.
- **Mindfulness and Emotional Acknowledgment:** Finally, being mindful of each other's feelings and needs, and acknowledging the growing distance, could have allowed them to address the issues early on.

Practical Ways to Soothe the Wounds Inflicted by Conflicts in Love

In the arena of love, we often bear the brunt of wounds unseen by the naked eye, wounds that embed themselves deep into the emotional fabric of our being. These injuries can linger, their sharpness as potent as the day they were inflicted, casting long shadows over our future relationships and coloring our outlook on love.

Whether you're nursing the raw hurt of a fresh breakup or dealing with the lingering sting of past conflicts, it's vital to remember this: Healing is not only possible; it is within your reach. The path to recovery may seem treacherous and tangled, but traversing it is the only way to emerge stronger, wiser, and open to love again.

Healing is not a passive process—it requires action, awareness, and a commitment to self-care. This journey is not about erasing the past or the pain, but about learning to carry those experiences differently. It's about transforming the hurt into wisdom and finding a way to make peace with your past.

The end of a relationship or the pain from conflicts in love can often leave deep emotional scars. Here are some practical ways to help heal these wounds and navigate the path towards recovery and resilience:

1. **Acknowledge Your Feelings:** One of the first steps to healing is acknowledging the pain. Understand that it's okay to grieve, to feel hurt and betrayed. It's part of the healing process. It's important not to suppress these emotions.

2. **Self-Care:** Take care of your physical health. Engage in activities that you love, whether it's reading, listening to music, hiking, or painting. Regular physical exercise can also be a great stress-reliever.
3. **Reach Out to Others:** Never underestimate the healing power of shared experiences. Reach out to your trusted friends and family, or consider joining a support group where you can talk freely about your feelings and thoughts.
4. **Practice Mindfulness:** This involves paying attention to the present moment, without judgment. This can be achieved through practices such as meditation, yoga, or simple breathing exercises. Mindfulness can help you stay grounded and avoid dwelling on past hurt or future worries.
5. **Focus on Personal Growth:** Look at the conflict or breakup as an opportunity for personal growth. Learn from the mistakes made and consider them as stepping stones to becoming a stronger, more aware individual.
6. **Therapy or Counseling:** If the pain seems too overwhelming, don't hesitate to seek professional help. A trained therapist or counselor can provide you with effective tools to handle your emotions and guide you through your healing process.
7. **Forgiveness:** This doesn't mean forgetting or justifying the pain caused. It's about letting go

of the resentment and anger that can hold you back. Forgiveness is more for you than for the person who hurt you.

8. **Rebuilding Trust:** If you choose to remain in the relationship after a conflict, rebuilding trust is essential. This involves open communication, transparency, and consistency. It's a gradual process but critical for healing.
9. **Cultivate Optimism:** Try to maintain a positive outlook towards life and love. Not all relationships are the same, and past experiences don't define your future ones.

Remember, healing takes time, and everyone's healing journey is unique. Patience, resilience, and self-love are key to soothing the wounds inflicted by conflicts in love.

Navigating the path towards recovery and resilience is more than just a checklist of practical steps; it's also about understanding the fundamental building blocks of healing. These blocks: honesty, trust, and vulnerability aren't just for rebuilt relationships; they're also vital components for personal recovery. As we've explored the practical steps of soothing wounds in love, it's now time to take a closer look at the importance of these building blocks and how they can fortify your healing journey.

The Healing Power of Honesty, Trust, and Vulnerability

Healing from heartbreak or a rift in a relationship is never easy, but it becomes possible with the powerful combination of honesty, trust, and vulnerability.

- **Honesty:** This is the starting point. Honesty means confronting the truth about the situation, even if it's uncomfortable or upsetting. It might mean admitting your own mistakes, or acknowledging that your partner wasn't who you thought they were. It can be a painful process, but honesty leads to understanding, and understanding is the first step towards healing. You need to be honest not only with your partner but also with yourself – about your feelings, your mistakes, your regrets, and your desires.
- **Trust:** The second ingredient in the healing process is trust. After a hurtful experience, trust can be hard to rebuild. It might be challenging to believe in love or even in your own judgment. Trust, however, is essential to moving forward. It's about trusting yourself first – that you have the strength to overcome the pain, and the wisdom to learn from your past. It's also about learning to trust others again, realizing that one bad experience doesn't mean everyone will treat you the same way. This doesn't happen overnight, but each small step of trust is a step towards healing.
- **Vulnerability:** The final component of healing is perhaps the hardest one: vulnerability. After you've been hurt, your instinct might be to close yourself off to avoid being hurt again. But shutting out the possibility of pain also shuts out the possibility of love. Being vulnerable means

opening yourself up again – to hope, to risk, and to connection. It means sharing your feelings, even when you're scared. It means admitting you need help, even when you want to appear strong. Being vulnerable is terrifying, but it's also liberating. It's what allows us to connect deeply with others, to truly give and receive love.

CHAPTER 7

The Art of Being a Conflict Warrior

"Turn your wounds into wisdom."

– Oprah Winfrey

From the boardroom to the living room, our lives are colored by varying degrees of discord, misunderstandings, and tension as seen and discussed up until now. But what if we could learn to not only manage but master these conflicts? What if we could become warriors in the face of relational challenges, turning obstacles into opportunities for growth? Welcome to the art of being a Conflict Warrior, a journey that doesn't shy away from difficulties but engages them with courage, compassion, and wisdom.

Understanding Conflict Resilience:

Conflict resilience refers to the ability to adapt and thrive in the face of conflict, rather than being paralyzed or defeated by it. It's a multifaceted skill set that involves emotional intelligence, clear communication, empathy, and a deep understanding of oneself and others.

The importance of conflict resilience cannot be overstated. In our personal relationships, it promotes harmony and deepens connections. In professional settings, it fosters collaboration and innovation. At its core, conflict resilience is about transforming potentially destructive forces into constructive and empowering experiences.

The journey to becoming a Conflict Warrior starts within the mind. It's about adopting attitudes and perspectives that are both proactive and compassionate.

- **Proactivity:** A Conflict Warrior does not wait for conflicts to escalate. They recognize signs early on and take initiative in addressing issues. This is about taking responsibility, not just for our actions but also for our reactions.

- **Compassion:** This involves understanding that conflicts often arise from misunderstandings, fears, and unmet needs. Approaching conflicts with empathy and compassion can lead to solutions that honor everyone involved.
- **Courage:** Facing conflicts head-on requires bravery. It's about standing firm in our values while also being open to the perspectives of others.
- **Growth Mindset:** Seeing conflicts as opportunities for growth and learning helps us to engage them positively. This perspective shifts the focus from winning or losing to learning and growing.

The mindset of a Conflict Warrior is not about domination or surrender but about balance, understanding, and collaboration. It's a journey that requires consistent effort and reflection, and it's one that leads to a more fulfilling and harmonious life.

Emotional Intelligence and Empathy in Conflict Resolution

Conflict is not merely an intellectual challenge to be solved; it's a human experience filled with emotions and intricacies. Therefore, understanding and navigating the emotional landscape becomes pivotal in conflict resolution. Emotional intelligence and empathy play a crucial role in this context, providing the foundation for effective communication, understanding, and collaboration.

Imagine you're in the middle of a heated argument, where the words are flying like arrows and the air is charged with tension. In the midst of this chaos, you,the Conflict Warrior, armed with the shield of Emotional Intelligence, begins to see not just angry faces but human beings, each with their unique fears, hopes, and desires.

You don't just hear words; you listen to the emotions beneath them. You sense the fear masked as anger, the longing hidden in accusations, and the love trapped within the walls of pride. This is the power of Emotional Intelligence, the ability to navigate the stormy seas of emotions without losing oneself or sinking the ship of relationships.

Emotional Intelligence and Empathy are not mere concepts but living practices, pathways that lead to the heart of conflict resolution. They teach us to see beyond the surface, to reach out beyond our boundaries, and to find solutions that honor not just our needs but the shared humanity that binds us all.

Imagine a world where conflicts are not wars to be won but bridges to be built, where differences are not threats but opportunities for growth. That's the world the Conflict Warrior seeks to create, wielding the twin powers of Emotional Intelligence and Empathy. It's a world where the heart's wisdom guides the mind, and compassion lights the way.

Emotional Intelligence and empathy are not inborn traits reserved for a few. They are skills that can be cultivated through practice, awareness, and commitment. Here's how one can develop these skills:

- **Practice Active Listening:** Truly listen to understand, not just to respond. This means being present, avoiding interruptions, and reflecting back what you've heard to confirm understanding.
- **Cultivate Self-Awareness:** Regular reflection on our emotions, reactions, and behavior in different situations increases our understanding of ourselves. This self-awareness is foundational to Emotional Intelligence.
- **Develop Compassion:** Regularly practicing compassion towards oneself and others can cultivate empathy. It's about recognizing the shared human experience and treating others with kindness, even in disagreement.
- **Seek Professional Guidance if Needed:** Workshops, books, and professional coaching can provide targeted support in developing these vital skills.

You can learn to listen with your heart, to understand even when it's hard, and to find solutions that resonate with love and respect. It's not a path free of challenges, but it's a path filled with richness, connection, and the joy of truly understanding and being understood.

Strategies for Thriving Amidst Relational Challenges:

In the heart of Kolkata, lived two families – the Boses and the Sens. For generations, they had been best friends, neighbors, and business partners, running a textile factory that had become a symbol of their unity.

However, a new business opportunity arose that drove a wedge between them. Mr. Bose saw an opportunity to modernize the factory, while Mr. Sen was adamant about preserving traditional techniques. They both believed that their approach was not just a matter of profits but a way to honor their heritage.

The disagreement escalated to a point where it threatened not just the business, but the families' relationship. The children, who had grown up playing together, were caught in a vortex of tension and animosity.

During a particularly heated argument in the community hall, Mr. Bose's daughter, Anjali, stood up. The room fell silent as she reminded everyone of their shared history, values, and the importance of the factory to the community.

Rather than taking sides, Anjali proposed a solution that would combine both modern and traditional methods. She suggested involving the community in the decision-making process, holding workshops, and forming a committee to find a common ground.

What followed was a series of meetings, discussions, and collaborations. The community came together, and their shared love for their craft led them to a solution that honored both innovation and tradition.

The factory thrived, and so did the friendship between the Boses and Sens.

The strategies for thriving amidst relational challenges are not secrets hidden away in ancient tomes. They are practical wisdom, timeless principles, and hands-on practices that anyone can adopt. It's a journey of turning obstacles into opportunities, chaos into creativity, and disputes into dialogues.

- **Embrace the Challenge**

  First and foremost, we must learn to embrace conflict as an opportunity for growth. When relational challenges arise, they bring with them the seeds of deeper understanding and connection. It's not about winning the battle but about growing through the struggle.

- **Listen and Understand**

  Thriving in conflict means listening with more than just our ears. It involves understanding the feelings, needs, and values behind the words. It's about hearing the unspoken, sensing the hidden, and touching the core of what truly matters.

- **Communicate with Clarity**

  Clear and compassionate communication is the cornerstone of thriving amidst challenges. Speak your truth but with kindness. Be assertive without being aggressive. Communicate your needs, but also remain open to the needs of others.

- **Build and Rebuild Trust**

  Trust is the foundation of any healthy relationship, and it's often the first casualty in conflict. Thriving means not only building trust but having the courage to rebuild it when it breaks. It's a process of transparency, consistency, and a commitment to healing.

- **Cultivate Resilience**

  Challenges will come, and they will go, but what remains is your inner strength and resilience. It's the ability to bounce back, to grow through the pain, and to find joy and wisdom in the process. Resilience is your inner compass, guiding you through the storms and leading you to the shores of peace.

- **Collaborate and Create**

  Thriving in relational challenges is not a solitary quest. It's about collaboration, teamwork, and the creative dance of finding solutions together. It's about turning adversaries into allies, problems into possibilities, and conflicts into collaborations.

- **Reflect and Learn**

  Finally, thriving means reflecting on the journey, learning from the experiences, and growing through the wisdom gained. Every conflict, every challenge, and every struggle has something to teach us. It's a mirror reflecting our strengths, our areas for growth, and the endless possibilities of human connection.

CHAPTER 8

Seeing Conflict through a New Lens

"The only way to make sense out of change is to plunge into it, move with it, and join the dance."

– Alan Watts

The clamor of disagreement, the sting of harsh words, the chasm of misunderstood intentions—conflict is often perceived as the destroyer of relationships and harmony. But what if we turn the kaleidoscope just slightly, allowing a different pattern to emerge? What if conflict, instead of being a dark cloud, is a transformative force—a prism that refracts relationships into their most beautiful colors?

Conflict is not the enemy we make it out to be. It's a sign of life, a pulsation of human existence that beats to the rhythm of our desires, fears, and ambitions. This chapter invites you to a journey, a discovery that unfolds the hidden opportunities behind conflict. A journey that paints conflict not as a deadlock but as a dance, a choreographed movement towards deeper understanding and growth.

Let's begin by exploring a new perspective, one that redefines the very core of conflict's inherent nature.

Understanding Conflict's Inherent Nature:

Often in life, we find ourselves locked in a battle, fists clenched, ready to fight our way through disagreement and discord. But what if the very act of fighting is what's keeping us from growth? What if we unclench our fists and open our minds to see conflict not as an obstacle but an essential aspect of growth?

Conflict is not a wall; it's a door. A door that leads to a deeper understanding of ourselves and others. It's an invitation to explore the hidden facets of our relationships and to discover the vulnerabilities and strengths that lie beneath the surface.

In the Indian context, conflict is often seen through a cultural lens that emphasizes harmony and unity. The shadow of disagreement is sometimes considered a sign of failure or weakness. But this view misses the true nature of conflict, a nature that is intertwined with the very fabric of human connection.

Conflict challenges us to confront our beliefs, our biases, and our fears. It forces us to look beyond the surface, to dive into the depths of our psyche, and to reflect on what truly matters. It's a catalyst that propels us towards growth, understanding, and transformation.

In redefining conflict, we begin to see it as a process, a dynamic interplay of forces that leads to change. We start to appreciate its role in shaping our lives, our relationships, and our communities. We recognize its power to stir, to challenge, and to invigorate.

This fresh perspective on conflict's inherent nature requires us to unlearn some deep-rooted beliefs and to embrace a mindset that celebrates conflict as a force for growth. It's time to step into the dance of disagreement, to move with its rhythm, and to allow it to lead us to a place of deeper connection and understanding.

By seeing conflict as a transformative force, we unlock its potential to heal, to connect, and to inspire. We begin to perceive it not as a problem to be solved but as an opportunity to be seized.

The Metamorphosis of Relationships

Metamorphosis – a profound change in form, a transition from one state to another. In the natural world, it's a process that turns a caterpillar into a butterfly, a seed into a blossom. Within the context of human relationships, it's a conflict that acts as this catalyst for transformation.

Imagine a relationship as a garden. In a garden, the soil must be tilled, seeds planted, and weeds pulled. Likewise, relationships require nurturing, care, and the occasional uprooting of thorny issues. Conflicts act as catalysts for deeper understanding and connection within relationships, akin to the gardener's spade that turns the soil, allowing fresh air, nutrients, and new growth to emerge.

Within the Indian cultural landscape, where family and social bonds hold a central place, conflicts are often swept under the carpet, hidden away for fear of disrupting harmony. However, this act of avoidance only buries the issues, letting them fester. Addressing conflicts, instead, lays the groundwork for trust, empathy, and mutual respect.

Take the example of a young married couple, both working hard in their respective fields. The stress of balancing work, family, and personal life leads to disagreements, misunderstandings, and frustration. But what if, instead of letting these conflicts drive them apart, they use them as opportunities to grow together?

Through open dialogue, empathy, and understanding, they delve into the core of their disagreements. They learn about each other's needs, fears, expectations, and dreams. They work together to find solutions, to build bridges over their differences. They become partners in the true sense, transforming their relationship from a battleground into a shared journey.

It's a dance, a movement where each step, each twist and turn, leads to a deeper connection and understanding. It's the art of turning conflict into collaboration, disagreement into discovery, discord into harmony.

Transformative Conflict in the Family

Family is a mosaic created with threads of love, loyalty, tradition, and sometimes, conflict. In an Indian household, where the family holds utmost importance, conflicts can be quite overwhelming and challenging.

But what if we look at family conflicts through the lens of opportunity? What if we see them as moments that can strengthen familial bonds, that can bring us closer together?

Consider the story of a family in a small town in India. The ageing parents, the responsible elder son, and the ambitious younger daughter, all live together, yet a chasm growing between generations. Conflicts arise over career choices, lifestyle preferences, and even simple day-to-day decisions.

Initially, these disagreements lead to tension, anger, and resentment. The family is at a crossroads, torn between tradition and change. But instead of allowing these conflicts to tear them apart, they choose a different path.

They sit together, talk openly, listen without judgment, and understand each other's perspectives. They recognize the fears, the hopes, and the dreams that lie behind their words. They see each other not as adversaries but as family, each with their unique viewpoint and value.

Through this process, they discover a new way of relating, a way that honours both tradition and individuality. They learn to appreciate their differences, to see them as strengths rather than weaknesses. The conflicts that once threatened to break them now bind them closer together.

The family becomes a symbol of what's possible when conflicts are viewed as opportunities for growth and understanding. It's a lesson in resilience, empathy, and love, a testament to the transformative power of conflict within the sacred space of family.

These stories and insights challenge us to see conflict not as a dreaded foe but as a friend, a guide, and a teacher. They invite us to embrace the dance of disagreement, to move with its rhythm, and to transform our relationships into something truly extraordinary. Whether it's a romantic partnership or the intricate web of family, conflict holds the key to unlocking the doors of understanding, connection, and growth.

The Prism of Conflict

Conflict, much like a prism, has the power to break down relationships into their fundamental components, refracting the light that binds us into its constituent colours. It exposes the spectrum of human emotions, revealing hidden facets of our connections. While it can be uncomfortable, even painful, it offers an opportunity to explore, understand, and ultimately, to grow.

Refracting Relationships

Think of a prism. When light passes through it, the light is refracted into a spectrum of colours. Similarly, conflict in relationships refracts our understanding, revealing hidden nuances, colours, and shades.

In the Indian context, where societal structures and expectations often govern relationships, conflict can be seen as a tool for personal insight. It's not just about winning or losing an argument but understanding the core beliefs, values, and motivations that underlie the disagreement.

Take, for example, a family dispute over a financial decision. On the surface, it may appear as a simple disagreement over money. But when viewed through the prism of conflict, it can reveal underlying issues of control, security, trust, and responsibility.

By breaking down the relationship into these fundamental components, we can gain deeper insight into ourselves and others, allowing for empathy, clarity, and resolution. Conflict, in this sense, is not a barrier but a bridge to greater understanding.

The emotions that arise during conflict are varied and intense. Anger, frustration, fear, sadness – these feelings can often overwhelm us. However, they are also a vital part of the human experience, reflecting the spectrum of our emotional landscape.

In a traditional Indian joint family, emotions are often closely interwoven. A simple disagreement can escalate into a turbulent storm of emotions, impacting everyone involved.

Understanding this emotional spectrum is key to navigating conflict constructively. It's about recognizing our emotions, accepting them, and expressing them in a way that fosters connection rather than division.

This emotional awareness, often rooted in practices like mindfulness and active listening, enables us to respond rather than react. It's about moving from a place of emotion-driven conflict to conscious communication, turning the heat of disagreement into the warmth of connection.

A Marriage Transformed:

In the bustling city of Mumbai, a young couple named Ravi and Meena faced a marital crisis. They were happily married, immersed in their careers and enjoying the vibrant energy of a city that never sleeps. Friends, family, and shared love for travel, and food filled their lives with joy and contentment.

Then came the call that changed everything. Meena received an incredible job opportunity in London – a dream offer but one that meant relocating to another country. Ravi's career was firmly rooted in India, and he had no desire to leave. The conflict seemed insurmountable. Arguments replaced the laughter, tension replaced the warmth, and a wedge began to drive them apart.

They knew they had to face this disagreement head-on. They decided to go on a weekend retreat together, away from the distractions of the city. The retreat was filled with emotional conversations as they shared their dreams, fears, values, and love for each other. They spoke openly and honestly, sometimes painfully so.

They realized that their relationship was more valuable than any job or location. They wanted to find a way to make it work, to honour both their desires and needs. After many heart-to-heart conversations, they found a compromise. Meena would accept the job in London, but they would make it a short-term assignment. They agreed on a time frame, and Ravi explored opportunities to work remotely.

Years later, they often reflect on that period as a turning point in their relationship. The conflict led them to a deeper understanding of each other. It tested their commitment and resilience but ultimately strengthened their bond. They emerged from the experience more connected than ever, now living their dream together in Mumbai.

They even began to counsel other couples, sharing their story and insights on how to use conflicts as opportunities for growth. Their story became a testament to the transformative power of conflict, a beautiful example of how a marriage can not only survive but thrive through challenges. Their experience showed that conflicts, however daunting, can lead to a deeper and more fulfilling relationship if handled with care, empathy, openness, and willingness to compromise. It's a lesson in how love can triumph over the most significant challenges, inspiring all who hear their tale.

This success story beautifully highlights the profound impact of conflict when approached with open-mindedness, empathy, and a commitment to personal growth. It defies the conventional narrative by showcasing the transformative potential of embracing challenges and seeking resolution.

CHAPTER 9

The Society's Script in Our Personal Drama

"Society exists only as a mental concept; in the real world, there are only individuals."

– Oscar Wilde

In the grand theatre of life, we frequently find ourselves playing roles not entirely of our own making. We receive scripts handed down through generations, rehearse lines steeped in tradition, and perform scenes expected of us. But what happens when we're trapped in a drama where societal norms and cultural expectations pull us in unwanted directions? Society itself often choreographs the conflicts that drive the narrative. In this chapter, we delve behind the scenes to explore how society dictates our personal dramas, how we navigate its rhythms, and how we can gracefully craft our own lines while still participating in the performance.

The Cultural Landscape

In a country where the community holds sway, personal conflicts often transcend the individual and become a matter of family, caste, or even neighbourhood. A disagreement between spouses may invoke the wisdom of elders; a business dispute might be handled within community councils. The societal script is often non-negotiable, with generations standing as both witnesses and judges.

The Family Script

In the traditional Indian family structure, the roles are clearly defined, and expectations are often set in stone. Familial expectations and generational beliefs contribute to the way conflicts are handled within the family. Parents have dreams for their children, grandparents have wisdom to impart, and children are taught to honour and obey.

But what happens when individual aspirations clash with family expectations? When a young woman wants to pursue a career path that's not aligned with her family's wishes? When a son chooses love over an arranged marriage? The family script, written over generations, doesn't easily accommodate deviations. These conflicts become personal dramas, played out in the living rooms and dining tables of homes across the nation.

Gender Roles and Conflicts

The influence of gender roles in the Indian context cannot be overstated. Men and women are often cast into roles defined by tradition, societal expectations, and sometimes even law. These roles influence conflicts, particularly within relationships and marriages.

In many parts of India, a woman's identity is intertwined with her family and later her husband. Her dreams, aspirations, and even grievances are often secondary. A husband, on the other hand, may be burdened with the weight of being the provider, protector, and upholder of family honour. When these roles are challenged or redefined, it leads to conflicts that are deeply personal yet societally scripted.

Community's Clasp: How Societal Ties Bind and Influence Our Personal Conflicts

In the densely interwoven fabric of Indian society, the community plays a pivotal role. Neighbours are not just people who live next door; they are often integral parts of one's social existence. Communities in India are tight-knit, offering support, friendship, and a sense of belonging. However, this closeness can sometimes translate into pressure and influence that shape personal and relational conflicts.

Consider the story of Priya and Karan, a young couple from a small town. They were deeply in love and wanted to marry, but there was one obstacle – they belonged to different communities. In their town, marrying outside one's community was more than just uncommon; it was taboo.

Their relationship was not a secret affair whispered in corners but a topic of discussion in the local tea stalls and community gatherings. The couple found themselves under a microscope, their every move watched, judged, and criticized. The community pressure was not just a distant murmur but a loud, clear voice telling them what was right and wrong.

Priya's friends advised her to think of her family's reputation, the community's honour. Karan's elders warned him of the consequences of breaking tradition. The love that once blossomed freely began to wilt under the constant scrutiny and judgment of the community.

They tried to fight, to argue that their love was their own, that they had the right to choose. But the community's script was not written by them, and its lines were delivered with authority and conviction.

In the end, Priya and Karan chose different paths, succumbing to the overwhelming community pressure. Their story is not unique; it's a narrative played out in many small towns and villages across India.

The community's influence in personal and relational conflicts is a double-edged sword. While it provides a sense of belonging and continuity of tradition, it can also become a restricting force, stifling individuality and personal choice.

Learning to navigate community pressure requires understanding its roots, acknowledging its power, and finding ways to assert one's autonomy without entirely severing the bonds that connect us to our social milieu. It is a delicate dance, one that demands courage, wisdom, and grace.

The delicate art of balancing societal norms lies in striking a harmonious balance between societal expectations and our own desires. Let's unravel this intricate dance into simpler terms, gaining insights into how to gracefully navigate this intricate terrain.

- **Finding the Right Balance**

  Imagine a young woman wanting to pursue a career that's traditionally considered suitable for men. How does she make her family understand her dreams without going against their values? The answer lies in honest communication, understanding both sides and finding a middle ground that respects individual dreams and family traditions.

- **Adapting to Changes**

  Society is always changing, and so are the rules that govern it. Being flexible means keeping up with these changes without losing oneself. It's about being open to new ideas and willing to adapt, but without compromising on what's truly important to you.

- **Building Strength to Handle Pressure**

  Life throws many challenges our way, and societal pressures can sometimes be overwhelming. Building resilience means having the strength to handle these pressures without losing sight of who you are. It includes having a support system of friends and family, taking care of yourself, and focusing on personal growth rather than seeking approval from others.

Navigating Professional Pathways

The professional landscape often serves as both a theatre and battlefield, where individual ambitions, societal norms, and personal values clash and coalesce. The story is not just of personal triumph or failure but how these professional encounters shape and are shaped by the complex cultural milieu.

- **The Corporate Ladder and Societal Gaze**

  Climbing the corporate ladder is often seen as a universal goal, but in many Indian contexts, the ladder may be steeped in tradition, community expectations, and family pressure. For instance, the choice of profession can be a matter of family honour rather than personal interest. An engineer in a family of doctors might experience a crisis of identity, caught between following his passion and aligning with family tradition.

- **The Glass Ceiling and Gender Roles**

  In many workplaces, the glass ceiling isn't just a barrier to professional growth for women but a reflection of societal gender roles. The unspoken expectations of a woman's place in the family and her duties as a wife and mother often conflict with her professional aspirations. This friction can lead to an exhausting balancing act, seeking success in both personal and professional life without alienating family and society.

- **Workplace Harmony and Caste Dynamics**

  Even the modern office space is not immune to the historical and societal construct of caste. Caste-driven prejudices can infiltrate professional relationships and lead to conflicts that are not only personal but deeply rooted in history and society. Navigating these waters requires an understanding of not only professional decorum but the unspoken social dynamics that might be at play.

- **The Ethical Dilemma and Societal Values**

  The professional sphere is also a stage where ethical dilemmas can mirror societal values. Decisions about business ethics may resonate with deeper questions about one's place in the community and alignment with cultural principles. A business leader choosing between a profitable but unethical opportunity and a moral but less lucrative path might find himself wrestling with conflicts that go beyond business, touching the very core of his identity within his community.

- **Embracing Authenticity and Individuality**

  While the intersections of professional life, societal expectations, and personal values can create complex conflicts, they also provide opportunities for growth, understanding, and authenticity. By recognizing and embracing these intersections, individuals can craft a professional path that doesn't just conform to society's script but reflects a more profound personal truth and connection to the community.

The dance of life within society is not about following a strict script. It's about understanding the rules, playing by them when needed, but also knowing when to follow your heart. It's a delicate balance that requires awareness, adaptability, and resilience.

In a society as diverse and rich as ours, this dance becomes even more complex. But with the right approach, it's possible to maintain personal integrity while living up to societal norms. It's not about conforming but about harmonizing, not about losing oneself but about finding a way to be true to oneself within the community.

The dance continues, and each one of us has a unique role to play. By understanding the steps and learning to move with grace, we can all become adept dancers, enjoying the dance rather than tripping over the steps. It's about finding our rhythm and dancing to our own tune, even as we perform on a stage set by society.

CHAPTER 10

The Final Bow and the Path Ahead

"The best way to predict your future is to create it."

– **Abraham Lincoln**

Visualize your relationships as a vibrant kitchen, brimming with the sizzle, aroma, and vitality of culinary artistry. Each dish you craft with a loved one, friend, or family member becomes a distinctive recipe, harmonizing diverse flavors, textures, and ingredients.

Now, picture conflict as that unexpected spice, that surprising twist in the recipe. At first glance, it might seem out of place, too intense, or overpowering. But isn't it often the unexpected that brings excitement to a dish, that elevates it from ordinary to extraordinary?

As we prepare to close this book, think of this final chapter as the dessert course, a sweet yet insightful conclusion that will bring all the flavors we've explored together. We'll delve into practical tools and techniques—consider them your ultimate kitchen gadgets for conflict resolution. We'll explore the importance of self-awareness and reflection, the seasoning that enhances every relationship dish. And, we'll take a look at preparing ourselves for future conflicts, stocking our pantry so we're ready for whatever recipes life has in store for us.

Just like a great chef never stops learning, the lessons we've covered are lifelong skills that require nurturing. So put on your apron one last time, as we make our final bow and look towards the path ahead.

Now, picture conflict as that unexpected spice, that surprising twist in the recipe. At first glance, it might seem out of place, too intense, or overpowering. But isn't it often the unexpected that brings excitement to a dish, that elevates it from ordinary to extraordinary?

Think of those heated discussions with a friend as the sizzle of garlic hitting a hot pan, an initial burst of intensity that soon mellows into a rich flavour. Or those tough negotiations with a partner as the careful balancing of sweet and sour, finding the perfect harmony of tastes.

Even those full-blown arguments, those clashes that seem to set everything aflame, are like flambéing a dish. It's dramatic, it's fiery, but it's also a transformation, a rapid, intense heat that burns away the superficial, leaving behind something more profound, more nuanced.

Sure, there will be mishaps along the way. You might add too much salt, overcook the pasta, or even burn the sauce. But that's where the real cooking begins, where the real relationships deepen. It's in the adjustments, the tasting, the adding a pinch of this or a splash of that. It's in the laughter over a shared mistake, the collaborative effort to save a dish, and the joy of creating something beautiful together, even out of seeming chaos.

The kitchen of relationships is an ever-evolving adventure, a place of experimentation, learning, and growth. Conflicts are not mistakes in this kitchen; they are opportunities for creativity, for connection, for finding new recipes that satisfy both the heart and the palate.

Life is filled with unending challenges, unexpected twists, and surprising discoveries. Just when you think you've understood a particular aspect of your relationships, something new emerges, and you find yourself navigating a fresh terrain.

Perhaps you've just come through a complex conflict with someone close, or you're facing a decision that might alter your relationships in significant ways. The journey of relationships is intricate, but remember, every step you've taken has led you here, to a place of newfound understanding and strength.

As you stand at this juncture, ready to move into the next phase of your life, let these insights guide you:

- Life may present you with unforeseen challenges, but it's within these unknowns that you'll find your most profound growth. Embrace the uncertainties, and let them lead you to new insights and understanding.
- You've learned so much about yourself, uncovered hidden aspects of your emotions, and navigated complicated conflicts. Trust in this wisdom. Trust in your ability to handle whatever comes next. Your intuition is your most reliable guide.
- Don't go through this alone. Reach out to those around you, share your experiences, and listen to theirs. The connections you make can be a source of strength, comfort, and insight.
- Remember to enjoy the process itself, not just the destination. Find satisfaction in learning, in deepening connections, even when the path seems difficult.

The journey never truly ends. There will be more conflicts, more challenges, and more opportunities for personal growth. Keep moving forward, keep learning, keep growing.

"With courage in your heart and wisdom as your compass, the journey ahead is not a maze to escape but a landscape that holds invaluable lessons, boundless love, and infinite possibilities."

www.ingramcontent.com/pod-product-compliance
Lightning Source LLC
La Vergne TN
LVHW091105150826
845673LV00002B/723

* 9 7 9 8 8 9 0 6 7 9 2 8 4 *